An Introduction
to
Commemorative Medals

W. Wyon/Domard (*rev.* after H. Bonnardel): Great Exhibition, Council Medal, 1851

An Introduction
to
Commemorative Medals

Christopher Eimer

London

To Emily and Nicola

© Christopher Eimer 1989
First published 1989

Typeset by Enset (Photosetting), Radstock Road, Midsomer Norton
Printed in Great Britain by
Biddles Ltd, Guildford Surrey
for the publishers
B.A. Seaby Ltd.
8 Cavendish Square
London W1M OAJ

Distributed by
B.T. Batsford Ltd.
P.O. Box 4, Braintree, Essex CM7 7QY

ISBN 1 85264 031 6

British Library Cataloguing in Publication Data
Eimer, Christopher
An introduction to commemorative medals.
1. British commemorative medals, to 1983–collectors guides
I. Title
737'.222'0941

ISBN 1-85264-031-6

Contents

M. Fountain: 'Monumenta', 1985

Acknowledgements

Graham Dyer, Librarian and Curator of the Royal Mint, has given generously of his time during the writing of this book and has drawn my attention to several sources of information. The British Museum's Department of Coins and Medals has also been of much help. Missi, my wife, read the manuscript and has given me several ideas and suggestions.

R. Elderton: Edward Elgar, 1984

Introduction

Commemorative and historical medals, sometimes referred to as medallions, have their origins in late fourteenth-century Italy. Despite this long tradition, the art of which is today practised in many parts of the world, medals remain largely undiscovered, often being confused with those given for war service, campaign or gallantry medals, or merely dismissed as large-size coins.

Medals have been made in Britain since the sixteenth century. During the seventeenth and eighteenth centuries they excited comment in literary circles, with poets such as John Addison, John Dryden and Alexander Pope being among several to eulogize upon them. Their appreciation and study was also enshrined by a number of prominent collectors, such as Sir Hans Sloane (64), the eminent physician, whose collection of several thousand European medals, together with his books, manuscripts and curiosities, were purchased by the nation after his death in1753, forming the nucleus of the British Museum. The collection built by the anatomist William Hunter (73), although considerably smaller, has close parallels with that of Sloane. In 1783 it too was bequeathed to a public collection, along with his minerals and books, thus establishing the Hunterian Museum at the University of Glasgow. Hugh Percy, 1st Duke of Northumberland, began a family collection of European sixteenth to eighteenth-century medals, many of which were purchased on his behalf by an agent in Europe during the 1750s and 60s, a practice common at this time. They were recently dispersed at auction and many now reside in the British Museum. So outstanding is the condition of medals from the Hunter and Northumberland collections that a provenance linking them closely, if not directly, with an original source is quite clear. George III was one of the few royal collectors of medals. Accumulated through the exchange of gifts, and by purchasing agents, they were deposited in the British Museum after his death in 1820. Today, many of these medals still remain with their original paper roundels, on which are inked the king's monogram. Sarah Banks, sister of the naturalist Sir Joseph Banks, also formed a significant collection of medals, bequeathed to the British Museum and the Royal Mint after her death in 1818.

The first book in English to be devoted largely to the subject is that of the diarist John Evelyn, whose *Numismata, A Discourse of Medals*, written in 1697, discusses those medals made during and after the Renaissance, as well as including chapters on Greek and Roman coins. The medallic nature of classical coins, and their influence in the development of the Renaissance medal, account for the use of the word in this broader context; one which continued during the eighteenth and nineteenth

1

centuries, both in academic and commercial circles. Evelyn's diaries make clear his interest in antiquities and medals and several points of contact gave him insights into general areas of numismatics. He suggested, for example, that the inscription 'Decus Et Tutamen' ('An ornament and a safeguard') be placed on the edge of the first milled crown coinage of 1662.

One of the first books to deal with a particular aspect of medals, an approach ahead of its time, was George Vertue's work of 1753 on the seals, dies, coins and medals of Thomas Simon, one of Britain's most outstanding medallists (*see* **fig. 1**). In 1762, Francis Perry published plates containing illustrations of rare and celebrated medals, as did the numismatist Thomas Snelling in 1776 (**68**). In 1790 the first edition of John Pinkerton's *Medallic History of England to the Revolution* was published, dealing with medals up to 1688. The Royal Numismatic Society was established in 1836 (originally the Numismatic Society of London, until designated 'Royal' in 1904) and has included many significant papers on medals in its journal, the *Numismatic Chronicle*. During the nineteenth century, a number of personal accounts of medals and their makers were published, including those of Nicholas Carlisle on the medallist William Wyon in 1837; Edward Thomason, the Birmingham medal manufacturer, who published his memoirs in 1845; and Richard Sainthill, whose *Olla Podrida*, of 1844 and 1853 (2 volumes), is filled with copious notes about medals and medallists and reveals a close association with Leonard Charles Wyon, who engraved Sainthill's medallic portrait in 1855.

Edward Hawkins' *Medallic Illustrations* was published in 1885. It was

Fig. 1 Stuart?: Thomas Simon

based on the medals in the British Museum (where he was Keeper of Antiquities from 1826 to 1860) and those in other collections, and was supplemented by folio volumes of plates issued between 1904 and 1909. Despite a somewhat chequered history prior to publication, as outlined in the preface, it is the single most important work to have been written on British medals and after 100 years remains a standard and dependable work of reference. Leonard Forrer's encyclopaedic *Biographical Diction-ary of Medallists*, published 1904–30, is the largest general reference of its kind. The early part of this century saw the establishment of the British Numismatic Society, which has published important articles in the *British Numismatic Journal*. During the last twenty-five years a large number of books and papers have been written, both of a specific nature, such as Laurence Brown's *British Historical Medals*, as well as more general intro-ductions. The formation of the British Art Medal Society in 1982 has seen a greater awareness focused on medals, the interest in which has now begun to gather pace.

This book, while itself an introduction, attempts to present a fresh approach to British commemorative medals. It addresses the questions of definition, how and why medals came about, and the processes of manu-facture. Their formative years on the Continent are then briefly looked at, followed by a discussion of the medal in Britain. A following chapter cov-ers the different types of subject-matter which medals embrace, of which those examples given largely come from the British series, alone compris-ing more than ten thousand different types. The final chapter discusses the study, collecting and purchase of medals today, and deals with other attendant questions.

No attempt has been made to provide a critical analysis of medals or medallists, although general remarks have sometimes been irresistible. Similarly, opinions concerning the rarity of medals have for the most part been avoided. Unless otherwise stated, medals referred to are struck and not cast, and are contemporary to the period or date which is commemor-ated. When the description of a medal is not accompanied by a medallist's name the medal is unsigned. For expedience, copper and bronze, which are similar in appearance, are referred to as bronze. Most of the illustra-tions are actual size, although some only show one side of a medal. The values which accompany the list of illustrated medals are intended as an approximate and comparative guide. The Glossary will, I hope, deal with questions which the simple, but perhaps unfamiliar, terminology poses.

I trust that there is a sufficiently large and essential body of information with which to spark an interest in the subject. Medals do, after all, allow the excitement of discovery and provide information which can be of interest and value in so many spheres, yet they remain largely ignored. For me they have long been the source of surprise and curiosity, not to mention pleasure.

Chapter 1

What is a medal?

A medal can bring to life a particular event or character from history or it can be regarded simply as an individual work of art. The elements of design and form are most often contained within an object of handy proportions, one usually made of metal. This is a somewhat general and imprecise definition, but it does accommodate the medal's various functions. It also, necessarily, takes account of its rapidly changing and innovative forms which, over recent years, have been very imaginative. Despite this evolution, which today has secured for medals a place as a medium of sculpture, they have never strayed sufficiently far from their original form to entirely lose their identity. According to the *Oxford English Dictionary* the word itself derives from the Latin word for metal, 'metallum'.

The medal is a product with a distinctly European tradition, whose birthplace is Renaissance Italy. This was a time and a place which saw the emergence of an enlightened society, whose people found a gratification and a perpetuity of themselves through the medal, expressing the identity and hopes of its patrons – patricians, nobles and princes – in this new beginning. Expressions of art or symbols of achievement were nothing new, and it would be wrong not to acknowledge the influences, both in the medal's art and its imagery, which have come from Greek and Roman coins, some of them in the form of medallic presentations. However, the manufacture of an unofficial medal by one 'private' citizen for the gratification of another would then not have been tolerated, and in this respect at least the climate of Renaissance Italy was quite different. Furthermore, as the medal did not possess authority as a medium of exchange (the primary distinction separating it from coins), it was allowed to flourish, free from government control or interference.

While medals are not the most dramatic legacy of the Renaissance, they are amongst its most durable and intimate relics. Today they provide a rich source of personal portraits and devices, and capture the beauty of the period. The preservation of the portrait and the desire for immortality has been, in great part, the medal's *raison d'être*. To be slipped into the pocket, to hang around the neck or to lie upon the table, the medal is as personal as it is immediate. Mannerist and baroque medals of the sixteenth to eighteenth centuries continued to give precedence to the portrait, and while subsequently this has remained its most dominant feature, other considerations have come to influence its roles and the direction of its development.

Since those times, medals have been produced both by governments and private bodies, a mutual co-existence which has promoted their development, free from the forms of censorship imposed on 'conventional' sources of information, such as pamphlets and newspapers. The art of the medal has itself remained largely unfettered by restriction, with medallists usually having a completely free hand. Some even went so far as to introduce portraits of themselves on officially-commissioned work, 'concealed' amongst figures in a design, such as William Wyon, who cheekily included himself on the reverse of a life-saving medal as the figure pulling a survivor out of water (**266**). In contrast, the closely-related skills of the coin engraver are inhibited. Protocol usually governs the position of the sovereign's portrait on coinage, while practical considerations of design govern the relief, which has to be limited, so as not to cause undue wear while in circulation.

There are several ways in which and reasons why a medal comes into being: by a government or state, perhaps to celebrate a coronation or some other event; by an institution or society, as a prize or to honour an individual; by patronage of the medallist; as an expression of art by the medallist; and as a financial speculation by a medallist or a publisher, to commemorate and exploit an event of current interest. The sources of commissions and their frequency were influenced by the period, and many have resulted from an open competition whereby artists were given a brief and then submitted designs. The medal has gradually evolved with the times and has been used in various ways, particularly as an instrument of propaganda, with which to commemorate and satirize.

Casting and striking are the two primary processes used in the making of medals. Essentially, the cast medal is produced from hot metal and a mould, while the struck medal is the product of a metal blank having been impressed with a die (*See* **fig. 2**). The details of both processes are outlined in the Glossary. The technique of casting was the one first used to make medals, while striking in relief was introduced with the development of the screw-press in the early sixteenth century. Medals made by the two processes are different in appearance, most noticeably in their surfaces: those of cast medals have a roughness and flaws which, although variable, can be usually detected on close examination of the field; while those of struck medals are usually perfectly flat and clean.

Casting has always been a manual procedure, as was once that of striking. However, the introduction of steam-powered machinery in the late eighteenth century mechanized the production of struck medals, increasing output dramatically and rendering obsolete the screw-press. The development of the reducing machine in the nineteenth century and the advance of modern technology have resulted in the mass-production of

Fig. 2 Thomas Simon's die (*rev.*): Charles II 1661 coronation medal (**137**)

struck medals. Striking removed much of the medallist's individuality, which casting preserved, although at no time has it heralded the death of the cast medal. Today, medals produced by both techniques have, in their own ways and with their own devotees, come to assume equal prominence. There are several additional methods of making medals. The techniques of cameography, electrotyping, engraving and repoussé, all of which occupy a relatively small niche in the genre, are dealt with in the Glossary.

Copper and lead, and alloys such as bronze, brass, pewter and white metal are the most prolific metals used to make medals. They have also been made in gold and silver, although, like those in other precious metals, these are always liable to be melted down for their intrinsic value. Other metals in which medals have been struck, but less frequently so, are aluminium, iron, palladium and platinum. The purity of silver medals struck in Britain since the nineteenth century is usually of .925 (sterling) fineness, while that of gold is more variable, with privately-made medals up to *c.* 1900, and all Royal Mint official medals, usually of 22 carat. Under the 1973 Hall-marking Act, medals in precious metals have been required to be hall-marked.

Medals presented by institutions and societies as prizes are usually made of gold, silver and bronze, while those issued by local authorities to celebrate a monarch's jubilee or coronation were usually struck in white metal or bronze; examples in silver or gold possibly served as presentation pieces, perhaps for civic dignitaries. Other factors influenced the use of certain metals. For example, during the First World War, Trinity College Dublin not only awarded bronze medals in place of gold, but called upon recent recipients to contribute their gold medals (**260**) to the war effort, also to be replaced by medals in bronze, the exchange noted on the edge.

The development of different alloys provided a greater flexibility for medallists. Pinchbeck, an alloy of about five parts copper with one of zinc, with characteristics of brass, was developed in the 1730s by Christopher Pinchbeck, a clock and toy manufacturer. It saw considerable use in the mid-eighteenth century as a metal from which medals could be cheaply produced, although the fabric was quite susceptible to corrosion. The use of lead, white metal and pewter (an alloy of tin and lead) became widespread during the eighteenth century, although these metals were also susceptible to corrosion. In an attempt to maintain a more stable fabric, thereby limiting deterioration of the metal, a small plug or core of copper was inserted into many eighteenth-century pewter medals during manufacture. The practice seems to have been most prevalent on the Continent, particularly in Germany, although it was not entirely successful. During the nineteenth century improvements were made in the constituents of base metal alloys, although there still occurred a good deal of variation with many medals sufficiently soft to be bent effortlessly, while others, with an alloy of different proportions, being considerably tougher. The difference to the naked eye between a silver and a white metal medal, especially when in fresh condition, is not always obvious. Medals made of the base metals will only give a muted or 'dead' sound when struck on the edge by a metal object, as distinct from those made of gold, silver, bronze, or other 'hard' metals, which will, when so struck, usually emit a long 'ping'. In addition, the design of base metal medals, being rather soft, will often be somewhat diffused or ill-defined on the very highest points of the relief.

Berlin iron, which has a particularly fusible quality suitable for casting delicate and fine objects, was used for the making of uniface medals (carrying the design and lettering on one side only), principally in Germany during the early nineteenth century. These medals, which comprise a portrait gallery of eminent European contemporaries, are typified by characteristics of a black or almost-black colour, and a slightly grainy surface.

Copper medals sometimes received a superficial bronze coating which could vary considerably. It could, for example, take the form of a purple wash consisting mainly of oxide of copper; a patina which was formerly imparted to the copper by heating it in contact with oxide of iron. But one of the most common forms of embellishment on medals is that of gilding, normally achieved through a chemical process using a gold amalgam. The techniques varied, although it was usually applied to the metal blank before striking. Some of the finest examples of gilding occur on bronze and silver medals produced at Matthew Boulton's Soho Manufactory in the late eighteenth and early nineteenth centuries. So effective could the process be that it can delude some into believing a medal to be of gold, although its purpose was usually to decorate and not to deceive. At any rate, both the factor of weight and the examination of the points where rubbing or a scratch may have occurred, usually on the relief, in the field, or on the edge, should betray the underlying metal. Generally speaking, medals in bronze and silver are those most commonly gilded.

A medal which has been parcel-gilt, or damascened, only has its relief – portrait, design, and lettering – gilded, thereby providing a striking and attractive contrast with the field, which is given a contrasting dark-brown patination. The process was used mainly on the Continent during the eighteenth century, but to a limited extent. Such medals rarely survive in superb condition, with their gilding completely intact.

Medals of the last hundred years or so were sometimes made with a coating of oxidized silver. Once again, points of contact, such as the relief or the raised rim of the edge, usually reveal the underlying metal, which is very often bronze. This silvering is particularly prevalent on French medals *c.* 1880–1920, which often carry a designation of the metal (such as 'argent' or 'cuivre') on the edge. In England, oxidized coatings were most commonly used by private medal manufacturers in the 1930s.

During the nineteenth century, an application of 'frosting', not unlike the icing on a cake, was given to the surface of some medals, especially those issued as prizes by clubs and societies. It was invariably applied to silver medals, which were then encased within two watch-style glasses or 'lunettes' and bound around the edge by a circular silver band. A treatment used by the Royal Mint from the 1890s created a matt surface, which was preferred by some engravers as it did not reflect light in the way that a usual mirror-like surface would. The 1897 diamond jubilee medals and successive jubilee and coronation medals made by the Mint, except those of the present reign, were given this finish, as was the 1902 'proof' coinage for the coronation of Edward VII. In the 1920s the Royal Mint employed a range of surface treatments, as had been in use at the Paris Mint, whereby a variable toning, sometimes almost black, was introduced by means of a French lacquer. The techniques used in the sixteenth century for the coating of medals are given in contemporary accounts, such as that of Benvenuto Cellini, one of the more celebrated practitioners. Old and modern techniques are more recently discussed, respectively, in Hill/Pollard, *Medals of the Renaissance*, and Hughes and Rowe, *The Colouring, Bronzing and Patination of Metals*, London, 1982.

Unlike coins, the art of enamelling has been practised on medals to a very limited extent. Their high relief posed difficulties of a practical nature, while their size made them unsuitable for wear as brooches, a use to which enamelled coins were frequently put in the late nineteenth century.

Although really outside the scope of this book, it is interesting to note the many materials other than metal which have been used to make medals or medallic forms. Those in ivory include portraits of European contemporary and historical figures, many made *c.* 1690–1710, in an oval form. An interesting series of French ceramic portrait medals of contemporary figures was made by Jean-Baptiste Nini during the second half of the eighteenth century (*Jean-Baptiste Nini, Sa Vie-Son Oeuvre*, by A. Storelli, Tours, 1896). A large number of Wedgwood ceramic oval medals were made, comprising portraits of eminent people (*Wedgwood, The Portrait Medallions*, by Robin Reilly and George Savage, London, 1973). Ceramic medals were made extensively in Germany *c.* 1920–40, commemorating events of political and social interest.

Several series of wooden medals were made in Germany during the sixteenth–eighteenth centuries, many to be used as draughtmen's pieces, and based on contemporary medals (*Spiele*, catalogue of the Bavarian National Museum, by Georg Himmelheber, Munich, 1972). Bois Durci, a black composition consisting of, amongst other things, sawdust and albumen and developed in the 1850s by Charles Lepage of Paris, was used to make a series of uniface portrait medals of famous mid nineteenth-century people (*see* **fig. 3**), (*Tunbridge and Scottish Souvenir Woodware*, part 3, by Edward and Eva Pinto, London, 1970). In the United States during the late nineteenth century, wooden medals commemorated events such as the centenary of independence in 1876 and the Columbian quatercentenary in 1892. To celebrate Queen Victoria's golden jubilee in 1887, medals made of black, brown, green and red vulcanite were produced by the India Rubber and Telegraph Works. In 1936, B.A. Seaby Limited produced a large bakelite medal to commemorate the abdication of Edward VIII, on which is recorded the full text of his farewell speech, broadcast to the nation from Windsor Castle on 11 December in that year. The medal has been frequently used as a novel

Fig. 3 Richard Cobden

Fig. 4 Box-medal: Wellington's Peninsular victories

form of advertising. One soap manufacturer produced medals in that material to commemorate the Festival of Britain in London, 1951. Other less
usual materials to have been used include amber, glass, horn, leather and
stone.

Many medals were made with the intention of being worn. This is usually made possible by means of a suspension loop or clasp attached to the
edge. An early and decorative example takes the form of a continuous
ropework border, usually in silver or gilt silver, to which is attached a suspension loop. These can be found on medals of James I for the peace with
Spain in 1604, and also on German 'gnaedenpfennig', or presentation
pieces, *c.* 1580–1650. Suspension loops attached to the edges of Civil
War and Royalist Stuart medals can be ornate, and the latter sometimes
occur with a pearl suspended from a loop on the bottom edge.

Medals in the form of circular metallic boxes, made either from medals,
or taking a medallic form, were made largely in the eighteenth and
nineteenth centuries. The lids, comprising the 'obverse', would be made
slot or screw into the main portion of the box, the bottom of which is the

'reverse'. Box medals usually contain engraved card discs or small medals, which commemorate historical series such as the British royal family and views of the Regency and, most commonly, events such as British naval and military victories between 1794 and 1815 (*see* **fig. 4**). International exhibitions held during the second half of the nineteenth century were often commemorated by souvenir box medals, usually containing printed views of the exhibition itself.

Medals have traditionally been circular in shape, and with two sides, although oval, square, rectangular, semi-circular and other less usual forms have also been made, depending on both the period and purpose. Developments in the art medal over the last twenty or thirty years have, however, severed all the old conventions governing shape. Today, artists freely explore the potential which the medallic form offers and are, in many cases, creating some extraordinary and exciting images.

Chapter 2

The medal in Europe: its formative years

Foremost among the makers of the first Italian Renaissance medals was Antonio Pisano, known as Pisanello, a portrait-painter from northern Italy. An accomplished artist skilled at drawing both the animal and human form, Pisanello was responsible for a group of more than twenty cast medals *c*. 1438–50. He usually signed his medals 'Opvs Pisani Pictoris', indicating his profession of painter and drawer (**1,6**). Today he is recognized as not only one of the first but also as one of the greatest of medallists.

There followed in Italy a number of craftsmen, many of them sculptors, who responded to the challenge of medal-making. Regional schools were formed, such as those at Carrara, Ferrara, Florence, Mantua, Milan, Rome and Venice, each the exponent of a particular style. Among the more prominent medallists are Matteo de' Pasti (**2,3**), Sperandio of Mantua, Niccolò di Spinelli, Giancristoforo Romano, Gianfresco Enzola (**4,5**), and Giulio della Torre (**7**). Their medals were made by the casting process from models usually made of wax, and are mostly of lead or bronze, often pierced at the top to enable suspension.

The Renaissance spread throughout Europe during the latter part of the fifteenth century, and with it went the art of medal-making, arriving in France, Germany and Holland at about the same time. Developments during the fifteenth and sixteenth centuries, from the Renaissance to the mannerist medal, were encouraged by changes in medallic technique; for example, wood or stone, rather than just wax, was now being used to make the models. The high-point of medallic art in the Italian Renaissance, the period 1440–90, is typified by large-size portrait medals, the reverses of which have high relief, lively and bold compositions and which sometimes incorporate the sitter's personal device. Italian mannerist medals, the peak of which were made in the years 1530–80, are prettier and more delicate in style, with perhaps more elaborate and refined reverses. At no precise point, however, is the division between the two styles absolutely clear.

The ability to strike a medal in relief was developed in the 1530s, following the introduction of the screw-press. Up to then, except for a small number of 'flat' or low relief medals, the technique of casting was the only one used. The two processes demanded quite different skills and

PLATE 1

PLATE 2

medallists tended to practise either one or the other. Benvenuto Cellini, a master goldsmith, who is credited with having perfected the screw-press, promoted the use of dies and struck a number of medals in the 1530s. A fashion for Roman coins at this time inspired medallists such as Valerio Belli, Giovanni del Cavino and Alessandro Cesati. As well as medals, they struck imitations of Roman sestertii, sometimes referred to as 'Paduans', after the home town of Cavino and Alessandra Bassiano, his collaborator in their production. Among the more prolific sixteenth-century Italian medallists are Pastorino de' Pastorini (**8,9**), Antonio Abondio (**10**), Pier Paolo Galeotti (**11**), Leone Leoni (**12**), and Jacopo da Trezzo (**13**). Both Abondio and Trezzo worked in northern Italy and Holland, the former also working in Austria and Germany. Pastorino produced a large number of charming uniface portraits.

The origins of French medallic art go back to the beginning of the fifteenth century, with two large-size cast medals of the Roman and the Byzantine emperors, Constantine the Great and Heraclius. There is no trace of Classical or Renaissance influences in the style of these medals, which seems to hang in the medieval-gothic period. A small group of medals *c.* 1450-60 commemorate the expulsion from France of the English. They are struck in very low relief, and owe their manner of execution to a coin-engraver and not a medallist. The Renaissance proper reached France at the end of the fifteenth century, when both Flemish and Italian medallists were at work, a geographical north–south divide separating the two. In Lyon, a contrast is provided between the work of a few Italian medallists, whose roots quite clearly lie in the Italian Renaissance, and that of French medallists, whose work seems to have had quite different origins. The very large bronze medal of Louis XII and Anne (**14**), for example, celebrating her entry into Lyon in 1499, where it was cast, although showing some Renaissance influence also has a heavy and cluttered style. Lyon continued for a time to be the centre of medal-making, where a number of struck, low-relief portrait medals were made as presentation pieces, as were other cast medals, some of which were beginning to reflect further outside influences. One of the more prominent French sixteenth-century medallists was Étienne de Laune, engraver at the Mint, who produced both cast and struck medals, *c.* 1550–70. The end of the century, however, saw the emergence of William Dupré and Jean Warin, whose work – mostly cast portrait medals, several of them large-size – established both at the forefront of medallic art in Europe in the early seventeenth century.

Albrecht Dürer, the celebrated Nuremberg painter and woodcut engraver, provided, through his drawings, the inspiration for a few medals, although he does not appear to have made any medals himself. In Germany, the formative period of medal-making covers the years *c.* 1510–90, and its two main locations were Nuremberg, centre of the goldsmiths' industry, and Augsburg, where many of the artists were sculptors, painters, woodcut engravers as well as goldsmiths. Amongst the most prolific German medallists were Hans Schwarz, Christopher Weiditz, Mathes Gebel (**15**), Hans Reinhardt the Elder (**16**), Joachim Deschler, Valentin Maler (**17**) and Baldwin Drentwett. Sources of patronage which medallists received were those of merchants, town burghers and noble families, whose portraits and coats of arms they recorded. Other materials, in addition to bronze and lead, were now being used by these medallists, such as silver, wood and stone, and the combination of new skills and new materials introduced novel dimensions to medal-making.

Quentin Matsys, the great Flemish artist, is generally acknowledged as the author of a small group of portrait medals, cast in lead and bronze *c.* 1490–1520 (**18**). The depth of these images is remarkable, but Matsys does not appear to have had any followers. Prominent among other makers of cast medals in the Low Countries during the sixteenth century were Jean Second, whose work is of bronze and lead; Steven van Herwick who produced medals in silver and lead, including portraits of English nobles (**19**), executed while he was in England; and Jacob Jonghelinck, a prolific medallist, who made medals of gold, silver (**20**) and lead. A group of late sixteenth and early seventeenth-century medals, struck by order of the provincial Dutch senates, are in low relief and usually without a portrait. Several relate to alliances with England, and the campaigns against the Spanish (**165, 206–7**).

PLATE 3

PLATE 4

Chapter 3

The medal in Britain

The Renaissance in Europe did not signal the existence of a great native British artist who could make medals, nor did it bring one with it. Only in the mid-sixteenth century is there any sign of a home-based medal activity, coming, without outside influences, from engravers of coinage at the Mint (designated 'Royal' *c.* 1810).

At this time, the position of medal engraver at the Mint was not official, nor one for which they had made any allocation. Such work was being executed by engravers, whose experience and skill had lain only in coinage work, with which the Mint had been successfully involved for many centuries. It was a well-structured organization with the Warden, Master and Comptroller at its administrative head, each of whom checked the work of various departments, such as that of the Chief Engraver who oversaw all aspects of engraving work, and the Assay Master whose concern was the fineness of metals. The tradition of shared responsibility helped to create a fail-safe mechanism, providing a security for the Mint's products, particularly its coinage, on which it was vital that the public could rely. At any rate, the characteristics of their first medals, of Henry VIII's Supremacy of the Church in 1545 and Edward VI's coronation of 1547 (**21**), do not disguise the origins of their makers. Cast, in low relief, and with a somewhat coarse design, they compare unfavourably with what was being produced on the Continent at this time (**11–13**). From these rather uncertain beginnings, the Mint has come to play an increasingly significant part in most aspects of medal design and production, at times comparable with, if not exceeding, the standards of other national mints.

Nicholas Hilliard, the celebrated miniaturist and goldsmith, may have extended his work to produce cast medals, possibly including those of Elizabeth I made after the Armada in 1588, and James I for the peace with Spain in 1604 (**22**). Developments began to take place, with medals now being struck, such as those for the coronation of James I in 1603 (**23**), for Henry, Prince of Wales, probably on his death in 1612 (**24**), and for a group of ministers and courtiers (**25**). They are reasonably well executed products of the Mint, in low relief, made by or under the office of Chief Engraver.

Despite these advances, the medal-making industry in Britain during the early seventeenth century was not yet self-sufficient. Nicholas Briot had been Chief Engraver at the Paris Mint, where he had already made a number of small-size medals. Disagreements with colleagues about his newly-developed techniques for striking, and the lack of patronage which these ideas received, forced him to England in 1625. He gained employment at the Mint in London, utilizing these new techniques which, amongst other things, produced coins and medals which were more perfectly round. Briot made more than twenty-five medals, many of a 25–33 mm diameter, relating to events in the reign of Charles I (**26–27**), including those for his coronations in London in 1626 and in Edinburgh in 1633 (**28**). Briot also made cast medals, the most significant of which commemorate Charles I's 'dominion of the seas' *c.* 1630. Two further medals, which occur both cast and struck and which commemorate the King's return to London from Edinburgh in 1633 (**29–30**) have been attributed to Briot. However their style seems sufficiently divorced from his signed work to suggest the hand of another Mint engraver.

Thomas Rawlins, an Englishman and ardent Royalist, was apprenticed to Briot and appointed engraver at the Mint in 1643, from which time he produced a number of cast oval Civil War medals, as well as those of Charles I, Henrietta Maria and Prince Charles for Stuart loyalists (**31–33**). From 1648–49, and from 1660 until his death in 1670, Rawlins occupied the post of Chief Engraver at the Mint and, following the Restoration, produced several medals for Charles II (**34–37**). Rawlins was also a coin and gem-engraver, as well as being a playwright.

The first highly-talented British medallists were the brothers Thomas (*see* **fig. 1**) and Abraham Simon (*see* **fig. 5**), born in England of French-Guernsey parentage. Abraham was an accomplished engraver and wax modeller, with approximately ten cast portrait medals bearing his signature (A.S.), as well as a number of wax portrait models, some for which no complete medals are known. Thomas was a coin, medal and seal-engraver whose greater medallic ouput includes approximately eleven cast and fifteen struck medals (usually signed T.S. or Tho. Simon). A number of unsigned medals can also be attributed to the Simons.

It would appear that Abraham prepared the wax models, while Thomas was the metal chaser for the cast medals and engraved the dies for the struck medals. However, it is possible that Abraham is wholly responsible for those cast medals which only he has signed; perhaps coincidentally, there appear to be no medals, cast or struck, made by Abraham after the death of Thomas in 1665. The Simons' cast and struck medals are highly-skilled productions and include portraits of Oliver Cromwell (**38**), Charles II (**137**), parliamentarians, noblemen and officers of high position (**39**). Thomas entered the service of the Mint in 1635 and studied engraving under Briot, eventually reaching the position of Chief Engraver in 1649. He was deprived of this office on the Restoration of Charles II in 1660, having found much favour under Cromwell's Protectorate, but was made Engraver of Seals in 1661. His earliest medal commemorates the Scottish rebellion in 1639 (**40**), and his last is that celebrating Charles II's

PLATE 5

PLATE 6

ABRAHAM SYMONDS. modeled in Wax
& Embossed of medals

C. Zretter p.   G. Vertue del.

Fig. 5 Abraham Simon

'dominion of the seas' in 1665 (**41**). The portrait on the latter is based on the celebrated 'petition crown' of 1663, which Simon presented (unsuccessfully) to the King for his judgement and comparison with another portrait submitted by the engraver John Roettiers. Abraham is recorded as working in England in the 1640s, having produced wax portraits on the Continent. He does not appear to have held an official position at the Mint, and it seems that he had another profession. In such a relatively short space of time, and during a period of such political upheaval, the quality of the Simons' work is considerable and stands quite alone.

For much of the latter part of the seventeenth century, medallic output is dominated by medallists from Holland, and in particular the Roettiers family. John Roettiers came to England with his brothers, Joseph and Philip, soon after the Restoration. He worked at the Mint for Charles II under Thomas Rawlins, whom he succeeded as Chief Engraver on the latter's death in 1670. Roettiers was from the start involved in coinage work, particularly in the preparation of the dies for the new milled coins, through which there existed much rivalry with Thomas Simon. Roettiers engraved the dies of more than forty medals, including the first large-size struck medals in England, principally of Charles II (**42–43**) and James, Duke of York (**44**). The medal issued for the Peace of Breda, concluded with Holland in 1667, is one of Roettiers' most common. The model used to represent Britannia, for the medal's reverse (**45**), was the celebrated beauty Frances Theresa Stuart (later Duchess of Richmond and Lennox). It is referred to by Pepys, who 'at my goldsmith's did observe the King's new medall, where in little there is Mrs Stewart's face as well done as ever I saw anything in my whole life, I think; and a pretty thing it is that he should choose her face to represent Britannia by!' (*Diary*, 25 Feb. 1667).

The 1670s and 1680s are a period greatly occupied by medals commemorating political intrigues and plots, some of which form the butt of contemporary satirists. The acquittal from treason in 1681 of Anthony Ashley Cooper, Earl of Shaftesbury, is commemorated by George Bower's interesting medal (*see* **fig. 6**), of which was written:

> One side is fill'd with Title and with Face;
> And, lest the King shou'd want a regal Place,
> On the reverse, a Tow'r the Town surveys;
> O'er which our mounting sun his beam displays,
> Five daies he sate, for every cast and look
> Four more than God to finish Adam took
> Cou'd it have form'd his ever-changing will,
> The various Piece has tir'd the Graver's Skill!

(John Dryden, *The Medall, A Satyre against Sedition*, 1682 (selected extracts)).

Fig. 6 Bower: Anthony Ashley Cooper, Earl of Shaftesbury

Bower had been appointed engraver at the Mint in 1664. His origins are uncertain, although an indenture of the Goldsmiths' Company, creating him freeman on 10 July 1667, merely refers to Bower as an 'alien'. He made more than forty medals, including those for the Restoration of Charles II (**46**), his marriage to Catherine of Braganza in 1662, as well as those concerning other affairs (**47–49, 169–174**).

Many of the medals produced in the late seventeenth century concern the birth of Prince James, the 'Old Pretender', in 1688, the flight of James II and the Protestant ascendancy of James' son-in-law and daughter, William of Orange and Mary, both in 1689, and the military campaigns in the 1690s. The majority of these medals were being made by Dutch medallists, most notably Regnier Arondeaux, Jan Boskam, Jan Luder and Jan Smeltzing, many relating to the accession of William and Mary (**50**). John Roettiers was eventually assisted at the Mint by his son Norbert who, together with his brother James, was appointed an engraver in 1690. They also made a number of medals relating to William and Mary, although it is unclear whether some are joint works or, if not, to whom they should be attributed. In 1697, following the discovery of dies which had been improperly obtained from Mint employees, John Roettiers was deprived of his office. The Roettiers, who worked in northern Europe during the seventeenth and eighteenth centuries, are one of the largest dynasties of coin and medal-engravers, exceeding in members, if not output, the Wyons.

As early as 1669, a Royal Patent gave certain engravers the right of the graving of dies for medals of any metal and the monopoly of medals bearing portraits of the sovereign, thereby restricting opportunities of counterfeiting. Under initiatives created by Isaac Newton, appointed Master of the Mint in 1699, and the shadow of the now numerous Continental medals, greater prominence was given at the Mint to the medal. There was

Fig. 7 John Croker

usually little work in coin-engraving alone, as the designs tended to remain the same, excepting the renewing of worn dies or the preparation of dies for a new reign. Good engraving work was considered the best security of the coin, and Newton secured the right of engravers to indulge in the making of and private trade in medals, so as to keep their hands in practice. A Royal Warrant of 2 November 1706 empowered officers of the Mint to:

> make and sell such medalls of fine gold & silver
> as does not relate to State affaires. . . And that you be
> further Impower'd to Direct and require the said Gravers
> . . . to make such other Medalls of fine Gold, fine Silver,
> and fine Copper with plain historical designs and Inscriptions
> in Memory of great Actions as shall be approved by you the
> said Warden, Master & Comptroller of our Mint. And to make
> Embossments, Puncheons, Dyes and other Instruments requisite
> for Coyning the same (PRO Mint 3/18).

The most prolific engraver at this time was John Croker (*see* **fig. 7**), a German whose father, Christoph, was a wood-carver. Croker came to England in the early 1690s and gained employment as a goldsmith with a London jeweller. He joined the Mint in 1696 as under-engraver to Henry Harris, and became Chief Engraver one year after the latter's death in 1705. Croker was in a position to take advantage of the new freedom accorded medallists and produced definitive portraits of Anne, George I and George II, as well as many medals commemorating the military campaigns and affairs with which Britain was involved (**51–53**). The design of his medal commemorating the Duke of Marlborough's victories in 1703 had created an unfortunate juxtaposition, by seeming to compare the equestrian figure on its reverse, assumed to represent Marlborough, with the portrait of Queen Anne on the obverse. This had caused embarrassment among Mint officials who were obliged to censor Croker's future medal work and required that medallists now sign all their work. Croker's preparatory designs were thus submitted for the approval of the Warden, Master and Comptroller, such as his sketch for a medal commemorating the revival of the Order of the Bath in 1725, with the charming depiction of little Prince William (later Duke of Cumberland) in the robes of the Order (*see* **fig. 8**).

The enlightened arrangement between the Treasury and the Mint was cleverly balanced. It ensured that there were engravers sufficiently skilled to undertake coinage work at a moment's notice, while at the same time allowing them, between such work, to usefully profit from the making and sale of their own medals. This was a desirable and necessary incentive, as the salary which coinage work alone commanded was insufficient to attract highly-skilled engravers. Under-engravers were also needed in

PLATE 7

44

45

47

46

48

49

50

PLATE 8

51

53

52

54

55

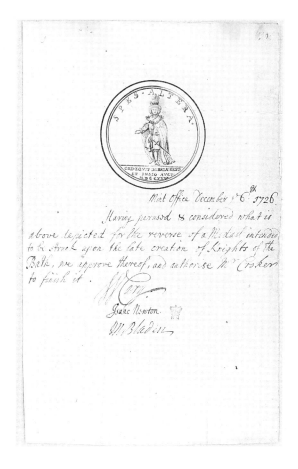

Fig. 8 Mint approval for a Croker medal

case of sudden departure, and a proposal in 1711 to engage an apprentice, Francis Beresford, provides an insight into this aspect of Mint administration (*see* **fig. 9**). Approval from the Treasury (10 July 1712) stated that Beresford was to be bound as an apprentice under Croker, who was to receive an annual allowance of £35 'for his care and training him up in the Art & Mystery of Graving' (BL Add. mss.18757).

Of the medals struck at the Mint under Newton's twenty-eight year Mastership, only three were official pieces, the rest, more than thirty-four, being sold for profit by the engravers. Most are by Croker, sometimes assisted by Samuel Bull, who had been taken on as an apprentice in the 1690s and whose initials appear on some of the reverses. The prices charged for these Mint medals, as itemized on two lists printed *c.* 1720 (*see*

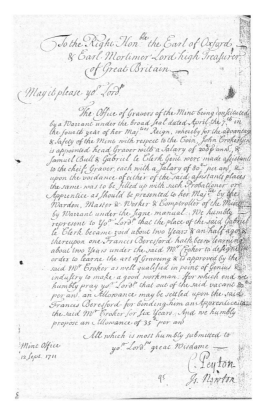

Fig. 9 Mint proposal for an apprentice

fig. 10) and *c.* 1732, relate directly to size and metal. On both, it is interesting to note the chronological placement of the second medal (**54**), in amongst those of 1702. Undated and unsigned, as is seemingly all of Croker's work commemorating events before 1704, it has usually been taken to commemorate the Union of England and Scotland in 1707.

Croker was not entirely satisfied with his lot, as is made clear in a petition to the Treasury in 1732, wherein he complains that since his appointment no provision had been made for the official employment of a smith or filer, payment having come 'out of my Sallary, with is now 36 years and reckon 25*l*. per annum one year with another amounts to 900*l*. . . . My petition is if their Lordships would please to allow 25 or 30 per annum for ye payment to such a person. That mans business is to smith, file, and polish the Dyes, and when the moneyers are a coining to attend and polish and clean the Dyes as often as it requires which is almost every hour in my day so that it is not an assistant to me alone but also to the moneyers' (BL

A L I S T of the M E D A L S ſtruck in the
Reign of her Late Majeſty, Queen *Anne*;
with their Price.

	In Gold.	Silver.	Copper.
	l. s. d.	*l. s. d.*	*l. s. s.*
THE Coronation Medal	3 15 0	0 5 0	0 1 6
A large Medal, the Motto, *Nova Palladium Troje*	30 0 0	1 17 0	0 17 0
On the taking and deſtroying the Galeons at *Vigo*	4 5 0	0 6 0	0 2 0
On taking *Keyſerwaert, Venlo, Ruremond,* &c.	4 5 0	0 6 0	0 2 0
The Queen and Prince	7 0 0	0 12 0	0 4 0
On the Surrender of *Bonn, Huy* and *Limburg*	7 0 0	0 12 0	0 4 0
The Chain of Hearts	3 15 0	0 5 0	0 1 6
Entirely *Engliſh*	3 15 0	0 5 0	0 1 6
On the Battle of Blenheim	3 15 0	0 5 0	0 1 6
On the Sea-Fight and taking *Gibralter*	6 6 0	0 7 0	0 2 6
On the Relief of *Barcelona*	3 15 0	0 5 0	0 1 6
On the Battle of *Rameilies*	3 15 0	0 5 0	0 1 6
On the Queen's giving the Firſt-Fruits and Tenths to the Clergy	8 0 0	0 12 0	0 0
The large Union Medal	8 0 0	0 13 0	0 4 0
A ſmall Medal on the Union	3 15 0	0 5 0	0 1 6
On the Battle of *Oudenard*	8 0 0	0 12 0	0 4 0
On the taking *Liſle*	8 0 0	0 12 0	0 4 0
On the Pretender's Invaſion of *Scotland,* in 1708	6 6 0	0 7 0	0 2 6
On the Taking *Sardinia* and *Minorca*	6 6 0	0 7 0	0 2 6
On the Surrender of *Mons*	6 6 0	0 7 0	0 2 6
On the Taking of *Tournay*	6 6 0	0 7 0	0 2 6
On the Battle of *Tannier*	8 0 0	0 12 0	0 4 0
On the Battle of *Saragoſſa*	10 0 0	0 15 0	0 5 0
On the Battle of *Almenara*	10 0 0	0 15 0	0 5 0
On the Taking *Douay*	10 0 0	0 15 0	0 5 0
On the Taking *Bethune, St. Venant,* &c.	10 0 0	0 15 0	0 5 3
On the Taking *Bouchain*	8 0 0	0 12 0	0 5 0
The Peace Medal	3 15 0	0 5 0	0 1 6
A large Medal on the Peace	20 0 0	1 5 0	0 10 0
	22 0 0	15 7 0	5 9 6

A L i s t of the M E D A L S ſtruck from
his Majeſty King G E O R G E's Acceſ-
ſion to the Throne, to the Year 1718.

	In Gold.	Silver.	Copper.
THE Coronation Medal	3 15 0	0 5 0	0 1 6
A large Medal on the King's firſt Arrival in *England*	30 0 0	1 15 0	0 15 0
On his Publick Entrance through the City	10 0 0	0 15 0	0 5 0
On the beating the Rebels at *Dumblain* in *Scotland*	8 0 0	0 12 0	0 5 0
On the Defeat of the Rebels at *Preſton*	8 0 0	0 12 0	0 5 0
On the Victory gain'd over the *Spaniſh* Fleet by Sir *George Byng* in the Mediteranean	8 0 0	0 12 0	0 5 0
On the King's being Mediator of the Peace between the Emperor, *Turks* and *Venetians*	8 0 0	0 12 0	0 5 0
			7 1 10

Note, *The Price of Gold Medals is according to their Weight,
ſo may be two or three Shillings more or leſs than what is
here ſet down.*

Fig. 10 Price list of Croker medals

Add. mss. 18757). Croker's petition was successful and led to the Mint appointment of the Surveyor of the Moneyers' Presses in 1734.

Croker's striking portrait medal of George II and Queen Caroline, with their children arranged on the reverse, by John Sigismund Tanner, may be the counterblast to Stuart claims of succession in the 1730s (**55**). Tanner, under-engraver to Croker, came to England from Germany in 1728. Through the new Master of the Mint, John Conduitt, he obtained a position, eventually becoming Chief Engraver on Croker's death in 1741. Most of Tanner's work was involved in the coinage of George II, although he did produce the Royal Society's Copley prize (**56**) as well as a silver medal (**57**), after a design by Hubert François Gravelot, for a lottery in 1736. The charges for Tanner's medal of John Milton (**58**), commissioned by William Benson, politician and critic, and struck in silver and bronze, outlines the stages of its manufacture and the respective costs (BL Add. mss. 18757):

	£	s	d
January 17th 1738			
50 copper blanks wt. 6¼ at 3d per lb.		18	9
15 days work prep. 102 blanks	1	17	6
To ye surveyor 3 days ½ at 5sh per day		17	6
To ye filer 3 days at 2sh 6d		7	6
To ye blancher 3 days ½ at 1sh 8d		5	10
To ye labourer 3 days at 1sh 8d		5	0
To coals, melting pots, Aqua fortis, Saltpetre and a copper pan		12	0
To 4 ounces of my own silver at 6sh	1	4	0
To an iron borer		10	0
To 2 outrings and six springs		4	0
To drawing ye copper to a proper size		2	6
To 8 dozen ½ of Shagreen cases at 10sh per doz doz	4	5	0
money expended	£11	9	7

The group of medals following the hopes of the exiled Stuart family, *c.* 1690–1780, form a continuous thread and can be seen as a means of keeping alive the Jacobite cause (**59–61**). Many are by Norbert Roettiers, who had left England in the 1690s and attached himself to the Stuarts in France. They include three uniform medals, but struck in different sizes, each with a bust of Prince James (*obv.*), who attempted a naval invasion of Scotland in 1708, and a map of the British Isles (*rev.* **61**), being the hoped-for restored kingdom of the Stuarts.

Jean Dassier, Chief Engraver at the Geneva Mint, came to England in 1731 and produced a series of thirty-four uniform medals of English monarchs from William I to George II (**62**). They were available on subscription, in silver at 15 guineas and bronze at 6 guineas, and were published with a descriptive list (*A Sett of Medals of all the Kings of England*, London, 1731). Dassier's son, James Anthony, worked at various European mints before coming to London in 1740, receiving the appointment of assistant engraver at the Mint one year later. He made a series of portrait medals of leading contemporary figures such as Edmund Halley, Alexander Pope and Sir Hans Sloane, most with only inscriptions on the reverse (**63–64, 244**). Lorenz Natter, a German medallist and gem-engraver, produced two particularly fine portrait medals of Charles Sackville, 2nd Duke of Dorset, in 1733, and Sir Robert Walpole in 1741, as well as coronation medals of George III and Charlotte of Mecklenburg-Stelitz in 1761 (**144–145**).

Admiral Vernon's victories in the 1740s were hailed by many medals, mostly struck in pinchbeck (**65**). The use of cheap pinchbeck, an alloy of copper and zinc, allowed medal-making to become a more egalitarian pursuit, one which began to embrace affairs at every level of society, and not just those concerning the State. Richard Yeo made two medals commemorating the battle of Culloden in 1746: one, in the form of a badge with a suspension loop, has all the appearances of having been conferred; the other, a portrait medal of William, Duke of Cumberland, was a private speculation, issued in gold (2 guineas), silver (1 guinea) and bronze (½ guinea). This medal does not seem to have been entirely successful, to judge from the sale of Yeo's effects (Langford's auction, London 2–3 February 1780, lot nos. 69–73) which includes over 160 examples. Yeo was appointed assistant engraver at the Mint in 1749 and succeeded Tanner as Chief Engraver in 1768. In addition to medals, he produced a number of admission tickets for the pleasure gardens at Vauxhall, but he is chiefly known for his work on George III's new coinage and as a founder member of the Royal Academy of Arts.

John Kirk was both a prolific medallist and a manufacturer of all kinds of metal-ware, judging from his trade card (*see* **fig. 11**). This gives no particular emphasis to his work as a medal-engraver, although the central device on the banner is loosely based on his medal of George II, possibly an apprentice piece, executed in 1740 when he was sixteen years old. Some of his medals (**66**), coin weights and advertising tokens (**67**) are not only

Fig. 11 John Kirk's trade card

signed but, unusually for an eighteenth-century medallist, also give an address (I. Kirk F. St Paul's Church-Yard). Kirk made over sixty medals (**68**) and was awarded premiums by the Society of Arts for medal designs.

The Society of Arts (or the Society Promoting Arts, Manufactures and Commerce, designated Royal Society of Arts in 1908) was founded in 1754. It sought to encourage medal work of a uniformly pleasing standard and, from 1758, awarded medals as premiums for work relating to their three primary interests. The first issue, designed by James 'Athenian' Stuart and engraved by Thomas Pingo (*see* **fig. 12**), was presented in gold and silver (**69**). The Society also wished to strike medals commemorating British overseas victories and offered a premium of 20 guineas for a copper crown-size medal with the best 'point of workmanship and boldness of relief by persons under the age of 25 [raised to 40 in 1762], after a model approved by the Society'. Stuart again provided sketched designs, including those commemorating the capture of Goree, Louisburg, Montreal (**220**) and Quebec in the years 1758–60. Dies were variously engraved by John and Lewis Pingo, Thomas' sons, who won premiums for this work in 1759–60 and 1761 respectively.

Encouragement of the arts by the Society has been and still is of continuing benefit to medallists. Those who won premiums for design and engraving in its early days include J. Kirk, G. Mills, T.R. Pinches, the Pingos, William Wyon, and his cousin Thomas Jr. Thomas Hollis, a patron of art, took an interest in the Royal Society of Arts and was himself spending large sums of money on the production and purchase of medals,

Fig. 12 Carwitham: Thomas Pingo

PLATE 9

PLATE 10

74

70

73

71

72

77

78

76

69

75

some of which he gave to institutions. At Ford's auction (in London, 17–19 May 1757) of the effects of the engraver and antiquary George Vertue, Hollis bought one group (Lot 36) containing several cast portrait medals by Thomas Simon, of whom Vertue had written a monograph in 1753, and in whom there was now considerable interest. Hollis had a deep interest in seventeenth-century republicanism and it seems likely that he or Vertue played a part in the manufacture of medals of Cromwell, his family and Parliamentarians (**70**), closely based on and imitative of originals by Abraham and Thomas Simon. Exactly who made them is not at all clear, although Forrer suggests that they are by James 'Athenian' Stuart.

Through his association with the artists Giovanni Cipriani and Stuart, Thomas Pingo received a number of medal commissions. He produced over thirty medals commemorating a wide range of subjects, such as King Stanislaus Augustus of Poland and Prince Charles, the 'Young Pretender', and was appointed assistant engraver at the Mint in 1771. Lewis, his son, succeeded to this position in 1776, and was Chief Engraver from 1779 until 1815, producing several innovative coinage designs, such as George III patterns and a set of maundy money, its numeral values of an unusual 'wire' form. Lewis Pingo also engraved some twenty medals, including a portrait of Captain Cook for the Royal Society, those of the numismatists Richard Mead and Thomas Snelling, and an undated medal of George III *c.* 1785, the reasons for which are not clear (**71**). John Pingo, Lewis' brother, engraved medals for the Royal Society of Arts (as did Lewis), although this is known only from the Society's records and not from his medals, all of which are unsigned. The brothers' trade card (*c.* 1780) advertises their services as engravers at a central London address, and either may be responsible for a number of unsigned medals from this period. Both Thomas and John also worked for the Goldsmiths' Company, engraving hall-mark punches for the Assay Office.

Calendar or almanack medals were being used from the late seventeenth century. One type comprises a circular disc, calibrated with days and dates, and fixed by a pin into the central well of the medal. A reading of dates is provided when the centre is aligned with calibrations on the medal's border. The more usual type has no movable parts and displays a tabulation on each side, indicating, respectively, the dates in each month on which a certain day falls and the phases of the moon (**72**). Most date *c.* 1730–1820 and were produced in Birmingham. They were usually made of brass, bronze or white metal, with the maker's name in a panel situated beneath the table of dates. These medals did not require particularly great skills in die-cutting, as would one with a portrait or design. In fact, the makers are little known as medallists and may well have worked in associated metal trades.

The pioneer spirit and romance of the late eighteenth century are recalled on many portrait medals, such as those of the explorer Captain

Cook (1784), the mechanical engineer Joseph Merlen (1785) and the scientist Joseph Priestley (1783). Political and social events are also well-documented, and include two medals of the 1770s, seemingly by the same hand, of Benjamin Franklin and David Hume. Edward Burch's full-bloodied medal of William Hunter is prominent amongst late eighteenth-century portraiture and a fitting tribute to the anatomist and collector (**73**). A group of medals by William Mossop, a prominent Irish medallist, commemorates figures in Irish political and social circles during the 1780s and 1790s, a number of which have no reverse. They include por-traits of the actor Thomas Ryder and the banker David Latouche; that of Henry Quin, a physician (**74**), was ordered directly from the medallist by Robert Watson Wade, a Treasury official, for presentation to Quin after Wade's recovery from illness. The growth of the agricultural industry can be measured by the large number of societies throughout Britain which began to award medals during the second half of the eighteenth century.

A partnership was formed in the 1770s between Matthew Boulton, medal-manufacturer and founder of the Soho Manufactory in Birmingham, and James Watt, who had recently invented a steam-powered press and whose patent Boulton managed to extend from 1769 to 1799. In 1788 Boulton turned his attentions to coining machinery, and in 1793 was joined by Conrad Heinrich Küchler, a Continental medal-engraver who came to work in England. The collaboration of Boulton, Küchler and Watt produced several well-made medals recording events in the reign of George III (**76**). The engineering capabilities of Boulton's Soho Manufactory in medal production are, themselves, the subject of an interesting medal (**75**), the reverse of which indicates how many coins of specific diameters could be struck in one minute by eight Boulton presses.

Boulton, together with Edward Thomason (formerly his apprentice), and George Collis (who took over Thomason's Manufactory), did much to establish Birmingham as a centre of medal production in the nineteenth century, second only to that of London. Thomason was as much an entrepreneur as he was an inventor, and the circumstances surrounding medals for the candidature of Henry Lascelles (*see* **fig. 13a**), William Wilberforce (*see* **fig. 13b**) and Lord Milton, as recounted in his memoirs, admirably demonstrate these facilities:

> In 1807 as I was on my road to Sheffield, a courier arrived at the inn, seemingly in great haste, and, changing his horse, informed me that Parliament was dissolved the night before. I was within twelve miles of Sheffield where I arrived in two hours. The contest for the county of York was spoken of as likely to be the most expensive that could be im-agined, the candidates being Lord Milton, Wilberforce and Lascelles. By that night's coach, I wrote to my establishment to get three sets of dies made for medals, the size somewhat larger than a dollar; to keep

the die-sinkers at work all night, when, by the morning's coach, they would receive from me what legend to put upon them, and the blanks could be got ready at the time, and to prepare for upwards of 20,000, with a hole in them for ribbons. This was done, and on the fourth day afterwards, just in time for the election at York, the medals arrived at Sheffield, about five or six thousand for each candidate. I proceeded with them to York, when the three committees took them all. Many hundred pounds was gained by this thought.

Fig. 13 Thomason's York election medals: (a) H. Lascelles (b) W. Wilberforce

The series of forty medals published by James Mudie and struck by Edward Thomason in 1820 is the largest of several to record British victories during the previous fifty years. Thomason was involved in the production of other large series of medals including his medallic bible, published *c.* 1830, numbering sixty medals contained in five volumes. Along with the impetus provided by Boulton's Soho Mint, a number of skilled medallists began to make their own mark in Birmingham at this time, including J. Westwood and J.G. Hancock, both of whom were succeeded by their sons; Thomas Webb, who contributed several medals to Mudie's series, in addition to engraving the dies for some thirty medals during the period 1800–20 including those of Nelson, Washington and Wilberforce (**191**); and Thomas Halliday, an engraver and die-sinker of medals and tokens, as well as a button-manufacturer, whose output of more than 130 medals, produced *c.* 1800–45, covers a very wide range of subject-matter, including that of Stonehenge (**77**).

A number of unsigned and undated early nineteenth-century medals *c.* 1810–40 provide information of current interest, such as a medal *c.* 1810 of the solar system which includes the discovery in 1807 of Vesta, the last of the four largest minor planets. Another illustrates the hemispheres, eastern (*obv.*) and western (*rev.*), showing the world as it was known *c.* 1820, with Australia, for example, identified by its former name of New Holland. A group of medals *c.* 1825, with a standard central cameo portrait of George IV (*obv.*), enumerate populations of countries, mileages from London, or a chronology of kings and queens, respectively. Linnaeus' recently-devised system of plant classification is illustrated on a medal *c.* 1830 (**78**).

The most celebrated medallists to emerge at this time were the Wyons, a large and prolific dynasty of engravers whose work, which included the engraving of coins, tokens and seals, was to dominate medal-making in Britain throughout the nineteenth century. The family was of German descent, the surname occurring on a medal of 1742, celebrating Emperor Charles VI's homage to Cologne. It is unclear whether this medallist and Peter George (II) Wyon, who is known to have been working then at the Cologne Mint, are one and the same person and, if so, whether he is the same person who came over to England in the 1740s or 50s. At any rate, the Wyons' genealogical table provides details of those working as medal-engravers in England.

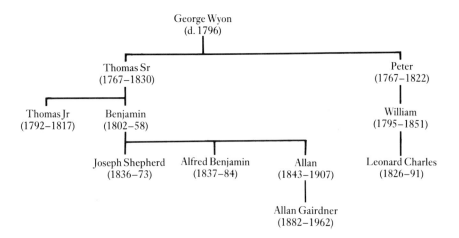

George Wyon is believed to be the first member of the family working as a medallist in England, and had a metal-engraving business in Birmingham. His sons, Peter and Thomas Sr, worked together as token- and medal-engravers, a partnership dissolved in 1800. Peter continued to work in Birmingham and engraved the dies for over twenty medals (**79**), while Thomas, who produced more than fifty medals, came to London and in 1816 was appointed Chief Engraver of Seals (not a Mint position). Thomas' first son, Thomas Jr, was an extremely talented engraver, who in his short life engraved more than twenty-five medals, some of a very high standard (**80**). He was apprenticed to his father in 1810, received a premium from the Royal Society of Arts for his work on their Isis medal (**252**), and in 1811 joined the engraving department of the Mint. His medal celebrating the visit to Britain of Grand Duchess Catherine of Oldenburg in 1814 (**81**) was struck at very short notice and to the same size and relief as the current 3s. Bank of England Token; it being necessary to strike the piece in one blow, as one could the token, thereby reducing the risk of damage to the dies. In 1815 he was appointed Chief Engraver at the Mint, but was to hold that position for just two years, until his death in 1817 at the age of twenty-five. Benjamin, Thomas' second son, also won premiums for medal work from the Royal Society of Arts, as well as from the Royal Academy of Arts. He succeeded his father as Chief Engraver of Seals in 1831, and engraved dies for more than fifty medals, including those for the Zoological Society of London (1826) and the opening of the Coal Exchange (1849), each with fine illustrations of their subject matter, the latter arguably his finest medallic work (**82**).

It was only in the early nineteenth century that the influence of neo-classicism was to make itself felt, chiefly through the work of William Wyon (*see* **fig. 14**) and Benedetto Pistrucci, between whom there was rivalry and bitterness. Pistrucci was a highly-accomplished engraver of gems, cameos, coins and medals who had come to England in 1815, having travelled to Paris from Rome, his place of birth. After it had been established that cameos which he had engraved *after* the antique were being sold as ancient and not contemporary pieces, he acquired something of a reputation, and was able to sell his gems and cameos for huge sums of money. Pistrucci's reputation was assured with his much-acclaimed St George and the dragon reverse for the new coinage of George III, which first appeared on the gold sovereign of 1817.

In an agreement of 1819 between the Royal Mint and Pistrucci (PRO Mint 3/21), a sum of £2,400, to be paid in instalments, was proposed for a large medal, to celebrate the recent victory at Waterloo. By 1849, when all but one (the Duke of Wellington) of the intended recipients had died, it still had not been completed. The idea of hardening the dies of this huge and elaborate medal in a form which allowed it to be struck was abandoned, and the piece only saw the light of day in electrotype (**83**) and

PLATE 11

79

82

84

81

83

80

85

PLATE 12

gutta-percha (the gum from the percha tree) form. Even though Pistrucci was already a highly-paid cameo-engraver, the sum initially agreed for his Waterloo medal, when it was at the preparatory stage of a model, is today difficult to reconcile. For the official coronation medal of George IV (**84**), Pistrucci had refused to use Thomas Lawrence's portrait, insisting instead on working directly from life, for which he was granted sittings by the King. His account drawn up by William Wellesley Pole, Master of the Mint, itemizes the various pieces of work and the respective charges (31 Dec. 1821, PRO Mint 3/22):

	£	s	d
For the invention & execution of a model in Wax with six figures allegorical of the Coronation of his present Majesty	105	0	0
For engraving D° in steel	525	0	0
For a Model and Engraving the head	157	10	0
For having changed the character of D°	52	10	0
For a second Model of the Head & Engraving	157	10	0
For having raised the figures of his Majesty in the reverse engraved in the year 1820 and for many other operations performed with great difficulty in another Punch in order to prevent a failure in the Work	157	10	0
For time employed in superintending the striking of the medals—for examining the same & for hardening all the Punches, Matrixes, & Dies which have been used	105	0	0

£1260 –

Comparisons in general need to be made between the fees and work of Pistrucci with that of William Wyon. Pistrucci produced only a handful of medals, including those of Wellesley Pole in 1823, George IV in 1824, the Duke of Wellington in 1841 and John Chetwynd-Talbot in 1853 (**85**). His compositions are a little harshly drawn, although his portraits display the clarity of a gem-engraver. This is noticeable on that of Queen Victoria, which was used on two coronation medals: the official Royal Mint issue (**146**), and a version, his largest struck medal, for the London manufacturing and retail jewellers, Rundell, Bridge & Rundell. This firm also commissioned medals by the Wyons for the accession and coronation of both George IV and William IV. Other jewellers to publish and retail medals during the first half of the nineteenth century include Hamlet, Hunt & Roskell, and Storr & Mortimer.

Fig. 14 William Wyon

William Wyon worked for and collaborated with his father, Peter, in the engraving of tokens and medals. In 1813 he received the Royal Society of Arts' premium for his work on their Ceres medal, the third family member to be so honoured, and began a career which was to establish him as one of the most prolific and skilled medallists of his generation. In 1816 he was appointed assistant engraver at the Mint under his cousin, Thomas Wyon Jr, but when the post of Chief Engraver fell vacant on Thomas' death, it was Pistrucci and not William Wyon who was considered by the Mint. Pistrucci's foreign nationality made him ineligible although, even with the post held in abeyance, he continued to receive its annual salary of £500, while not always performing its duties. He refused to copy Francis Chantrey's model for a medal, proposed but never struck, to commemorate the King's visit to Ireland in 1821.

In 1828 William Wyon was appointed Chief Engraver at £350 per annum, while Pistrucci, with political expedience, was given the newly-created position of Chief Medallist, his annual emolument now reduced from £500 to £350. Wyon had been performing the services of Chief Engraver but, unlike Pistrucci, had received a much-reduced £200 per annum. As compensation for those past services, he was paid a further

£500. The decision to strike a medal commemorating the coronation of William IV was made only a little more than one month before the event, to take place on 8 September 1831. In view of the shortness of time, it was suggested that William Wyon engrave the obverse and Pistrucci the reverse, a proposal which Pistrucci declined, feeling that there was insufficient time. The model for the portrait of William IV, by Francis Chantrey, was received by Wyon on 11 August 1831, and the work, for which he received £100 and which included his portrait of Queen Adelaide on the reverse, was completed on 25 August (**86**).

By most standards, William Wyon's output was prodigious; his medallic productions alone numbered more than 150, while his work on coinage was of equal, if not greater importance–mantles which were both to be assumed in equal measure by his son, Leonard Charles. As a medal-engraver, William had a freedom not enjoyed in coinage work and was at the Mint when the reducing machine was first introduced during the 1820s. This new device simplified the cutting of the actual-size die, which could now be done mechanically and directly, from the plaster or steel cast of the medallist's original model. As Chief Engraver, he was in a position to use the Mint's Great Die Press to strike private commissions, providing it was after normal working hours and without the assistance of men in that department. The making of private medals at the Royal Mint was a matter solely for engravers, work for which they received separate payment because it was outside the control of the Mint's chief officers. Medallists were permitted to sell replicas of their public medals in any metals, as well as to design and strike on their own behalf those medals which they considered worth making.

The first entry in a Mint ledger (30 May 1837) of William Wyon's private work (PRO Mint 3/28) records the striking of '20 silver medals of H.R.H. Princess Victoria'. A sitting for a Wyon portrait is in fact recorded in Victoria's published diaries (Saturday 27 April 1833), 'at 20 minutes to 3 I sat to Mr.Wyon to have my profile taken for a medal, till 10 minutes to 5' (*The Girlhood of Queen Victoria*, edited by Viscount Esher, vol.1, p.70). A later entry in the ledger records the striking of 2,288 medals between 30 May and 25 November of that year. Wyon's private medals sometimes carry certain designations, such as his medal of the architect Sir John Soane, which is inscribed 'Mint' beneath his signature under Soane's bust, the reverse with the façade of the Bank of England, one of his principal works. It was subscribed to and presented in gold to Soane in 1834 as 'a tribute of respect from British architects'. Examples were also struck in silver and bronze, and presented to the subscribers.

Significantly, changes to the Mint's Medal Department were being planned during the 1840s, including the termination of the right of private practice by medallists, whereupon medal work was placed under the control of salaried officers who were answerable to the Master. However, these changes were only implemented after William Wyon's death in 1851, allowing them to be wide-ranging and resulting in the virtual disappearance of private medal-making at the Mint. The Die Department was now charged with the manufacture of all Mint medals, including the large numbers of both the Naval and the Military General Service medals which were now being struck. Not until the 1920s and Deputy Master Johnson's administration was the making of private medals resumed to the same degree.

One of William Wyon's last commissions was for the conjoined portraits of Queen Victoria and Prince Albert (*see* **fig. 15**), to be used as the obverses for the Council (*see* Frontispiece), Prize and Jurors' Medals, awarded at the Great Exhibition in 1851. The Royal Commissioners of the Exhibition had offered three £100 premiums for the respective reverses, and those by H. Bonnardel (*see* Frontispiece), L.C. Wyon (*see* **fig. 16**), and G.G. Adams were chosen out of 129 designs. The other medals to be awarded, both by W. Wyon, were those for Services and Exhibitors (**87**). The Great Exhibition is also commemorated on numerous other medals, and gave rise to the many local exhibitions subsequently held throughout Britain, for which medals were also struck. The most eminent series of medals struck during the nineteenth century are those of the Art Union of London and the Corporation of London. The Art Union was founded in 1837 to foster and encourage interest in the fine arts, and sponsored the production of thirty uniform medals between 1842–87, each with the portrait of an eminent artist (*obv.*), and an illustration of his work (*rev.*) (**88**). Members paid an annual subscription for

Fig. 15 W. Wyon's unfinished plaster model: Great Exhibition medal (*obv.*)

Fig. 16 L.C. Wyon: Great Exhibition Prize Medal (*rev.*)

which they could choose either an engraved print or one of these medals in bronze, examples in silver being presented to artists and craftsmen whose goods gained the Council's approval. The Corporation of London also sponsored the issue of thirty medals; the majority by the Wyons and with diameters of 75 mm-80 mm. They relate to events in the City of London, such as the opening of buildings like the Coal Exchange (**82**) and the reception of British and foreign royalty. William Wyon's authoritative portrait of Victoria, which is the obverse for the Corporation's medal (**89**) commemorating her visit to the Guildhall in 1837, was used in 1840 on the first issue of postage stamps, the Penny Black. The Corporation's first medal commemorates the opening of London Bridge in 1831, and their last, the visit of Edward VII and Queen Alexandra to the City in 1902 (**163**).

Leonard Charles Wyon had become assistant engraver at the Mint in 1844. In 1851, on the death of his father and on the abolition of the post of Chief Engraver, he became non-resident Modeller and Engraver to the Mint, and produced over 120 diverse medals. The reverse of his medal of 'Father' Theobald Mathew, evangelist of temperance, has a group of kneeling figures receiving the pledge (*see* **fig. 17**), several of whom are identified in a letter (in the Birmingham Museum and Art Gallery) 'as all portraits from life . . . the boy was son of our gardener at Valebrook the young woman our pretty needlewoman Norrie Sullivan. The old men were my Uncle's men in the Yard, old Cody & Paddy . . . Who was the old woman I know not. Poor Norrie fainted while kneeling under her heavy cloak, so George my uncle's man, took her place and Wyon's sketch of her cloak with G's ugly bull dog head surmounting it was very droll' (dated July 14 ?, from Miss C.G. Saunders Forster, niece of Richard Sainthill,

Fig. 17 L.C. Wyon: ' Father' Theobald Mathew

to Ada ?). Leonard Charles Wyon was heavily involved in coinage and engraved the dies for the definitive 'bun head' penny of Victoria in 1860, a design which was to influence British bronze coinage for the following 100 years. In later years, he engraved dies for various commemorative (**90**) and prize medals struck by John Pinches for societies and institutions.

Pinches were a firm of medallists and die-sinkers established in the middle of the nineteenth century. Thomas Ryan Pinches, one of the first medallists in the family, had been awarded premiums in 1836–7 by the Royal Society of Arts for a medal design. He engraved a medal for the coronation of Victoria in 1838, one of his earliest, and produced a number in the 1840s. Others which he may also have subsequently made are signed only by surname, as are the majority of those produced by succeeding members of the family. John Pinches (**100**), after whom the firm came to be called, worked for the London medallist and die-sinker, William Joseph Taylor, who had set up a die-press at the Great Exhibition and struck large numbers of one particular medal commemorating the exhibition, with a bust of Prince Albert (*obv.*), and the royal coat of arms (*rev.*).

At the newly-erected site of Crystal Palace in 1854, it was Pinches who set up a press and struck medals, some of which occur in a circular, embossed metallic case bearing the firm's name.

During the second half of the nineteenth century, Pinches began to receive commissions from an ever-increasing number of organizations who wished to award medals. Until the medallist's right of private practice at the Mint was terminated in 1851, this work was being given to Mint engravers, and especially to William Wyon. Pinches employed successive members of the Wyon family, including Leonard Charles, Joseph Shepherd, Alfred Benjamin, Allan and Allan Gairdner. The Wyon reputation helped to establish and maintain the continuity of commissions which, at their height between *c.* 1880–1960, came from several hundred societies. Pinches also used the services of many other medallists, precipitated by the death of Allan Wyon in 1907, and their medallic output has been enormous. Unfortunately, it is on this altar that quality of design and engraving seems to have been sacrificed, particularly on their medals produced after the Great War and, in those respects at least, their work leaves something to be desired. During the 1920s, Pinches were involved in heated debate with the Royal Mint, the two in disagreement about monopolies and quality of workmanship, and after a period of intense 'investment' marketing during the 1960s the firm was finally sold.

The second half of the nineteenth century saw a huge increase in the numbers of medals being made, keeping pace with the growing demands and developments of an industrial age. Although many had very interesting subject-matters, reflecting these advances, the result of this mass-production was largely a loss of character on the medal itself. The demand was being met by an ever-increasing number of medallists and die-sinking businesses, many of them in Birmingham. Among the more notable are Allen & Moore, J. Davis, T. Fattorini, A. Fenwick, J.R. Gaunt, T. Halliday, R. Heaton & Sons, Hyam Hyams, J. Moore, J. & T. Ottley, J.A. Restall, J. Taylor, W.J. Taylor, and Vaughton. Their collective and most prodigious period of activity was over the years *c.* 1820–1930, during which time some were amalgamated or taken over. Ralph Heaton & Sons acquired some of Boulton's striking presses at an auction of the Soho Mint's effects in 1850, and became The Mint, Birmingham in 1889. J.R. Gaunt also made badges and related items, and used the medal both for self-promotion and to mark events of topical interest, such as the Test cricket series of 1928–9, and the flight of the *R101* airship in 1929. Thomas Fattorini Ltd tended to concentrate on badges, of which they produced a bewildering variety, and still flourish today as manufacturers of badges and regalia.

The first major reaction to the increasing numbers of struck medals occurred in the 1880s, with the establishment of the Society of Medallists. This sought a revival of the cast medal and the encouragement of all

Fig. 18 Legros: Charles Darwin

branches of medallic art. The movement was influenced chiefly by the artist Alphonse Legros, a Frenchman who had come to London in the 1860s and taken up the post of Slade Professor at London University. It was, however, the French sculptor and medallist, David d'Angers, who had already produced large cast portrait medals in the 1830s, and who was a telling influence in the development of the genre. Legros produced cast uniface medals of celebrated people of the day, such as Charles Darwin (*see* **fig. 18**), Lord Tennyson and John Stuart Mill, as did other artists, including E. Casella, F. Gleichen, E. Hallé, E. Lantéri and E.J. Poynter, some of whom had been Legros' pupils. Their legacy is a rich and varied portrait gallery of contemporary society, each hand-produced and with their individual treatment, which provides a light relief from the struck medal. Unfortunately, the early momentum which the Society achieved was not sustained and the Great War compounded its decline.

The jubilee celebrations of Queen Victoria in 1887 and 1897 are recorded on many medals, including large numbers of local issues, the first such occasions for which towns and districts struck medals (**91**). Many medals produced by private manufacturers over the years *c.* 1895–1915 carry a series of numbers, indicating a registered design, which protected the artist's work from unauthorized copying. A commonly-found example occurs on a medal made from the metal of Nelson's flagship

Foudroyant, produced in large numbers as souvenirs: with the designation 'Regd. No. 311430' at the bottom edge, below a uniformed bust of Nelson (*obv.*), and a ship at anchor, the inscription 'Foudroyant . . . wrecked at Blackpool June 16th 1897 / medal struck from copper of vessel after breaking up' (*rev.*).

The calendar medal began to be used for advertising purposes, with a tabulation of dates on one side, and a trader's name on the other. One such medal was issued during the 1850s by Moses and Son, a firm of tailors from London's East End. As the need for calendars diminished during the late nineteenth century, they were used more and more for advertising new products such as electric watches, telephones, typewriters and tyres. A much improved variation of the eighteenth-century rotating calendar was also being used in this way, but by the end of the First World War calendar medals had become obsolete.

Despite the large numbers of unimaginative medals being made in Britain, they continued to evolve on the Continent where many British sculptors had gone to study. The emergence of Art Nouveau towards the end of the nineteenth century was a development which returning English medallists, or foreigners coming to work in England, could respond to and interpret in their own way. Frank Bowcher studied sculpture at the National Art Training School under Edward Onslow Ford, a leading figure in the recently-formed 'New Sculpture' movement. Bowcher's early work, mostly commissions from Spink & Son, glory in the British Empire and the recent victories in the South African War. His national commemorative medal (**92**) was published in 1900 in the *Daily Mail*, along with Rudyard Kipling's specially-written war poem, 'The Absent Minded Beggar', and sold in aid of war widows and orphans. It depicts a standing figure of a soldier, his head bandaged (from Caton Woodville's painting 'The Gentleman in Khaki') (*obv.*), with the Union Flag and staff decorated with a rose, thistle and shamrock, the inscription recording 'the magnificent response of Britain's sons to the Empire's call to arms!' (*rev.*). One of Spink's earlier editions commemorates the 1890 jubilee of Rowland Hill's Penny Post (**93**). Many of their medals for the South African War were sold in aid of orphans' funds, such as F. Bowcher's medal commemorating the defence of Mafeking in 1900, which was issued in a case and sold for 12s 6d, one shilling of which was contributed to Lady Georgina Curzon's fund. Silversmiths and jewellers which published or manufactured medals in the late nineteenth and early twentieth century include Elkington's Garrard's, and Mappin & Webb.

Bowcher's medal for the Franco-British Exhibition of 1908 demonstrates the Continental influence in his work (**94**). While mildly French in sentiment, it recalls the influence of Anton Scharff, a prolific medallist of the Viennese school. Emil Fuchs, another Austrian medallist, came to England in 1897 from Italy where he had already gained a repu-

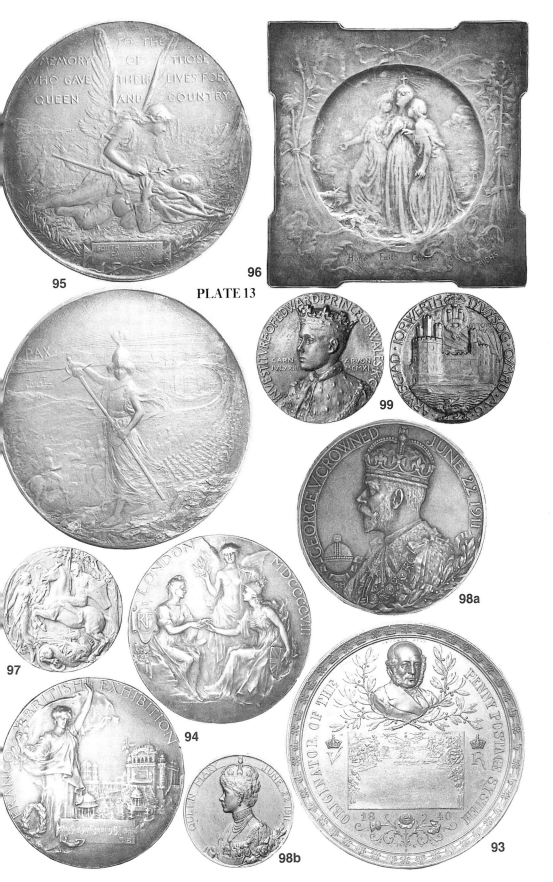

95

96

PLATE 13

99

98a

97

94

98b

93

PLATE 14

tation as a sculptor. He received several commissions, including a number from the Prince of Wales, for small portrait medals, sometimes set into ashtrays or other knick-knacks, to be given as personal mementoes. His medal for the South African War (**95**) strikingly contrasts the harshness of war with sorrow and pity; 'the sentiment', remarked Victoria to Fuchs about this medal, 'moves us deeply' (*With Pencil, Brush and Chisel, the Life of an Artist*, by E. Fuchs, New York, 1925). Perhaps his finest medallic work is that of Princess Alexandra, entitled 'The Princess of Pity' (*obv.*), with the figures of Faith, Hope and Charity (*rev.*) (**96**). It is a moving tribute, recalling the many causes with which she was associated, and displays a softness and grace, placing it at the very height of Art Nouveau on the medal in England. Fuchs was responsible for a number of other medals and worked on large sculpture, which took him to the United States in 1907, leaving behind a legacy of perhaps his finest medallic work.

Bertram Mackennal, the son of a Scottish sculptor, came to Europe from Australia and studied sculpture in Paris and London. His prize medal for the 1908 Olympic Games (**97**) demonstrates the sentiment of Art Nouveau in much the same way as Bowcher's Franco-British Exhibition medal. Mackennal's reputation was assured when called upon to design both the new coinage portrait for George V in 1910, a variation of which was used for the definitive postage stamps of the new monarch, and the official commemorative medal for the coronation (**98**). Unfortunately, the promise which he had shown, as seen on his Olympic medal, never came to be more fully realized in medallic form. He did, however, achieve fame as a sculptor, was subsequently knighted, and became the first overseas artist elected to the Royal Academy.

Members of the recently-formed 'new school' of sculpture looked to the possibilities of small-scale work, which the medal afforded. The most prominent, if not in this respect the most prolific, was Alfred Gilbert, whose model for a medal issued by the Art Union of London commemorates Victoria's golden jubilee in 1887. George Frampton, another member, had been greatly influenced by the Arts and Crafts movement, although techniques of repoussé and enamelling did not lend themselves fully to medals. One of Frampton's best-known medals is that commemorating the raising of the City of London Imperial Volunteers, commissioned by the Corporation of London and struck by The Mint, Birmingham.

The most prolific medallist of the 'new school' was William Goscombe John, a Welsh sculptor, who worked principally on large-size statuary and jewelled objects. Goscombe John entered the Royal Academy School in 1889 and won a travelling scholarship. While in Paris, he followed the working methods of contemporary sculptors such as August Rodin, and elements of this influence are visible in some of his work. His medal for the investiture in 1911 of Edward, Prince of Wales, stands quite apart from other contemporary medals in the way it embodies the qualities of 'sculpture in miniature'; an outstanding piece of work which, despite its appearance, is struck and not cast (**99**). Goscombe John received £262 for this commission, which served as the official Royal Mint issue. The investiture regalia, including the chaplet which the Prince can be seen wearing, was also designed by Goscombe John. Most of his other medallic work, however, arose from private commissions.

Despite this activity, there was insufficient momentum to establish a school of medal-making which could be compared to those on the Continent, particularly in Austria, Belgium, France and The Netherlands. The Mint, Birmingham, which executed the work of medallists such as Bowcher and Fuchs, remarked in a contemporary report that 'it is a matter for rejoicing that the medallist's art is in the course of transformation in England'. An optimism born, perhaps, more out of hope than of reality, for conservative British taste did nothing to remove an indifference to the medal and to the developments which were now occurring on the Continent.

There were isolated pockets of talent among British medal-makers, whose origins lay in the more formal nineteenth-century traditions of medallic art, as enshrined by William Wyon. George William De Saulles had trained at the Birmingham School of Art where the 1880 report records the award of several prizes for drawings from the life, and his first medallic work was for the firms of Pinches and Joseph Moore. Following the death in 1891 of Leonard Charles Wyon, De Saulles received the appointment of Engraver to the Mint with a fixed annual salary of £200. He engraved various medals, including a portrait of his former employee (**100**), but unquestionably his greatest legacy is the official coronation medal portrait of Edward VII and Queen Alexandra (**101**), and the uncrowned effigy of Edward VII (**102**), used for both coins and medals. The latter is a remarkable portrait, which in the course of time has lost none of its crispness. The premature death of De Saulles in 1903, at the age of only forty-three, deprived medallic art of a distinctive touch to portraiture.

The legacy of Oliver Sheppard, an Irish sculptor, is both as a medallist and teacher, and among his pupils numbered the future medallists Charles Leighfield Doman and Ernest Gillick. Sheppard executed a suite of four medals, awarded by Trinity College Dublin, in the field of medicine. Particularly interesting is that of the surgeon Edward Hallaran Bennett of 1906 which records, on the reverse, 'Bennett's' fracture of the metacarpal bone, as discovered by him. In Liverpool, the native sculptor and wood-carver, Charles J. Allen, made a distinctive medal commemorating the city's 700th anniversary of incorporation in 1907 (**103**), as well as others of local events and worthies. Allen's reputation as a wood and marble-carver is more prominent, and includes the panelling of ocean liners, very much a product of Liverpool, as well as the marble carvings on the reredos in St Paul's Cathedral. In 1907 Allan Wyon died, and with him the famous dynasty of medal-makers. Although his son Allan Gairdner was to continue, it was really all but in name, and he ran down the Wyon die-sinking business, farming out subsequent commissions to Pinches. He produced a small number of medals, including a memorial to his father, exhibited at the Royal Academy in 1908, and one of the benefactress Winifred Hardinge. In 1933 he entered Holy Orders, although he later submitted designs to the Royal·Mint, but without success. An aluminium medal, commemorating the loss of the *Titanic* in 1912, was sold on behalf of the Balham and Tooting Relief Fund: a broadside view of the four-funnelled passenger ship, and a plea 'Help Surpasseth Pity' (*obv.*), the inscription with dimensions of the ship, dates of sailing, and details of the disaster and location (*rev.*).

The number of medals produced in Britain during the First World War was very limited, in contrast to the Continent, particularly France, Belgium, and Germany. The German medals, many biting and satirical, were roundly condemned by *The Times*, which complained that 'those which have any claim to consideration as works of art can be counted on the fingers of one hand'. This paucity of medals in Britain, especially decent ones, prompted Sir Arthur Evans, President of the Royal Numismatic Society, to offer prizes in an open competition. *The Times* was enthusiastic, commenting that 'there are many signs that the problem of war memorials is exciting the serious consideration of those who are interested in the artistic side of the question, but none is more significant . . . than the announcement that the . . . President of the Royal Numismatic Society has offered prizes . . . for a medal to commemorate the Battle of Jutland'. The competition's brief required the production of a struck medal, without the help of a reducing machine; the steel dies were therefore to be directly engraved and made to the same scale as the model, of between two and three inches. Three medals shared four prizes, the obverse and reverse of one by different artists. The winning medal (**104**) was by Harold Stabler, a sculptor, and the runners-up were W. Gilbert, A.B. Pegram and C. Wheeler, who was to become President of the Royal Academy. In November 1917 a committee was set up by the Army Council to select the design for a general issue war medal. A Mackennal portrait of George V was used for the obverse and William McMillan's design, approved by the King, was selected for the reverse; its main feature, a horseman armed with a short sword, was, in the words of the artist, 'an allegory of physical and mental strength which achieves Victory over Prussianism' (**105**).

The First World War merely compounded the decline which had already begun, with neither medal competitions nor other initiatives sufficient to stimulate medallic art in Britain. By contrast, medal-making on the Continent was in a healthy state, with many mints enjoying a commercial interest, some with their own school of medallists.

The early 1920s mark the beginning of a period when medal-making in Britain experienced something of a revival, largely due to Robert Arthur Johnson (*see* **fig. 19**), Deputy Master of the Royal Mint, and the Royal Mint Advisory Committee. Johnson, aged forty-eight, already had experience in public administration when, in 1922, he took up his position at the Mint. In June of that year, the Royal Mint Advisory Committee was established to advise the Master of the Mint (Chancellor of the Exchequer) on all matters connected with the design and preparation of seals, coins, medals and decorations. It consisted of representatives from the Royal Academy, Royal Institute of British Architects, British Institute of Industrial Art, British Museum and Victoria and Albert Museum, together with one member nominated by George V, as his personal representative, and a consultant on heraldry.

Fig. 19 Robert Arthur Johnson, Deputy Master of the Royal Mint

Johnson looked at and compared the work of the Royal Mint with national mints on the Continent, such as those at Copenhagen, Paris and Utrecht. In the Mint Report of 1922, he emphasizes that his visit to Paris was of 'the greatest possible assistance to me in making my plans for our own Medal Department'. Having also looked at the work being produced in Britain by private medal-manufacturers, which he commonly referred to as 'the medal trade', he could see for himself the state of medallic art, and the malaise from which it was suffering. Johnson launched an attack against private medal-manufacturers who, it was now thought, had done little to raise the level of the art in Britain and had contributed to its decline.

Johnson saw the need to have a coterie of young artists able to produce medals, of which there existed few at this time. The right artists and a continuous stream of medal commissions would, it was hoped, result in trained engravers, who could at a moment's notice turn their hands to coinage work. This would be required on the accession of a new monarch, or if there was a decision to change the current coinage. (This did happen in 1927, when the silver coinage, which Johnson so disliked, was replaced by coins of new designs). Johnson was more at home in the atmosphere of a St James' club, than he was rubbing shoulders with artists, unlike Francis Derwent Wood, an influential member of the Mint's Advisory Committee and Professor of Sculpture at the Royal College of Art. Derwent Wood was well-placed to act as Johnson's talent scout and succeeded in introducing several young artists to medal-engraving, including J. Langford Jones, Percy Metcalfe and Thomas Humphrey Paget. With the powerful support of the Advisory Committee, Johnson now had the backing necessary to implement various changes to the face of the medal, as well as in the Mint's Medal Department itself.

In 1922, plans were drawn up for the British Empire Exhibition, held at a newly-prepared site at Wembley in north-west London, to encourage trade in the Empire and pay tribute to the colonial forces who had fought in the Great War. Johnson wrote to the Colonial Office in November 1922, stating that the forthcoming exhibition offered an opportunity for a commemorative medal which would be placed for sale, thereby giving employment to an artist and bringing his work to the notice of the public (PRO Mint 20/797). In May 1923 medallists from Britain and the colonies submitted designs for a medal and a plaquette commemorating the Exhibition. Prizes of £60 were offered by two city livery companies and the management committee of the Exhibition was to select the designs. The winners of the competition for the plaquette (**106**) and the award medal (**107**) were Edward Carter Preston and Percy Metcalfe, respectively; the latter with a representation of his 'Wembley' lion. Another of Metcalfe's designs won the first prize of £50 in the competition for the souvenir medal, to be produced at the exhibition itself: in low relief, florin-size, and capable of being struck with just one blow, at the rate of 105 a minute. At the age of fifteen, Percy Metcalfe (*see* **fig. 20**) had won a scholarship to Leeds School of Art, and this had led to a 'Royal Exhibition' scholarship at thge Royal College of Art. It was the British Empire Exhibition, however, which marked the turning point in his career.

The competition for the British Empire Exhibition medals had highlighted a growing controversy, with private medallists complaining that

Fig. 20 Percy Metcalfe working on a plaster model (of **117**)

the Mint was entering into direct and unfair competition with them. 'Contracts taken from private firms' was the headline of one letter from Pinches which was published in the *Daily Express* (23 November 1923). Johnson pointed out, in a letter (December 1923) to the Treasury, that the abolition of the post of Engraver in 1903 had enabled the Mint to approach outside artists for public work and, with the expanding use of the reducing machine, the Mint was able to strike medals for prices which were less than those quoted by private manufacturers. The Royal Academy, cited as one example, was paying more for its annual prize medals struck by Pinches than if it had gone to the Mint in the first place (PRO Mint 20/861). Johnson refers openly to the dispute (1923 Mint Report), stating his motives as 'directed solely towards the improvement of the ... standard of medallic art ... which will be of the greatest material benefit to the Trade'. In fact, correspondence with a prospective client (Dr Monckton Copeman, 27 March 1928) illustrates both Johnson's opinion of privately-made medals, and the zest with which he would pursue (in this case successfully) a commission:

> regarding the cost of producing a die it is, I am afraid, the case that our charges are higher than those which would be quoted by a private firm ... we give a great deal more care and attention ... to producing and finishing the dies and the medal ... In the ordinary trade they employ no artist at all and simply give a version for good or ill ... we submit

everything to the Advisory Committee. If you are considering Messrs Pinches, some of their work is tolerable but, as a general proposition, I would rather have a bath bun than the modern medal as struck by the British manufacturer, since the former would be much less deleterious to my digestion, delicate as it is, than the latter would be to my sense of taste (PRO Mint 20/1123).

In 1925 a deputation representing private medallists, chambers of commerce and the Royal Society of British Sculptors, saw the Financial Secretary to plead their case. After much negotiation, a compromise was reached whereby the Mint agreed not to operate a monopoly in connection with medal work. As far as privately-commissioned work was concerned, they agreed not to increase their staff and to handle, annually, an average of just eight pairs of dies, up to a maximum of fourteen. They also undertook not to use existing dies which had been made by private firms such as Pinches (PRO Mint 20/1003).

Metcalfe's official medal for the continuation of the British Empire Exhibition took as its theme food, transport and housing, the main interests upon which its extension into 1925 were focused (**108**). The design was as innovative and forward-looking as that on his 1924 medal. Metcalfe also received a commission for a medal which was to commemorate the Prince of Wales' forthcoming visit to Cape Town in 1925. It was one which, evidently, he considered important, writing to Johnson that 'I am particularly anxious to go all out on this medal' (PRO Mint 20/894). In fact, the medal was a success, with the Mint having received over 47,000 orders (**109**).

Correspondence between Johnson and Metcalfe certainly hints at a relationship of patron and protégé, and Metcalfe's portrait medal of Johnson's father (**110**), celebrating his eightieth birthday in 1925, could not fail to curry a little favour. His other notable medals from this period include the Carslake memorial of 1926 (**283**), King Fuad of Egypt's visit of 1927 and the Everest flight expedition in 1933 (**268**). Metcalfe, appointed 'Designer for Industry' by the Royal Society of Arts, was also active in other areas of design, such as shop fronts, environmental public areas, ceramics and even an ice ballet, which was produced each summer on Blackpool pleasure beach.

In 1924 the League of Nations wished to commission a medal and approached the Royal Mint. Four artists submitted work in a competition, each receiving an honorarium of six guineas. Carter Preston and Langford Jones were joint winners of the fifty-guinea prize, but the contractor could not come to terms with the League about its issue and it never passed the design stage (*see* **fig. 21**). At the British Empire Exhibition of 1924–25, a number of companies had medals struck by way of self-promotion, including Anthracite Collieries, Gibb's Dentifrice,

Fig. 21 Design for a proposed League of Nations medal

Mond Nickel Company, who produced a medal in pure nickel, and the Gramophon Company, whose ingenious piece, made in both aluminium and bakelite, simulates a miniature record.

Despite public indifference to the Mint exhibit at the British Empire Exhibition, new work was forthcoming. A medal was struck by the Mint for the London, Midland and Scottish Railway Company, to be presented to those who had given service during the General Strike in 1926. It was designed by Ernest Gillick, whose well-balanced composition hints at the Art Deco style, with a seated and helmeted figure of Britannia (*obv.*), and an allegory of three standing figures supporting a locomotive, the inscription incorporating the Company's initials (*rev.*). The Mint charge for the first pair of dies and preparation of punches was £52 10s., while the unit cost of manufacture was 2s. 6d. for the first 5,000, and 2s.4 ½d. thereafter. Approximately 7,750 medals were struck, each presented in a case together with a letter of thanks. One of Gillick's earlier medals, a Great War memorial for members of the Inner Temple, can also be singled out as progressive in design (PRO Miunt 20/1054).

In 1926 the firm of J.S. Fry Ltd, the chocolate manufacturers, decided to present a medal to the workforce on its bicentenary in 1928. The Royal Mint invited Eric Gill, Percy Metcalfe and Harold Youngman to submit designs, each to receive an honorarium of ten guineas. The Advisory Committee rejected the designs of Metcalfe, who was by now caught up in work for the Irish coinage. Eric Gill made a model in boxwood, but was asked to prepare a revised model, which was subject to much delay. Ultimately, it was Youngman's design which was the most acceptable and he received a fee of 70 guineas. Six thousand medals were struck in bronze, each with a dark toning, similar to that applied to Gillick's medal for the General Strike and Metcalfe's British Empire Exhibition medals (PRO Mint 20/1068).

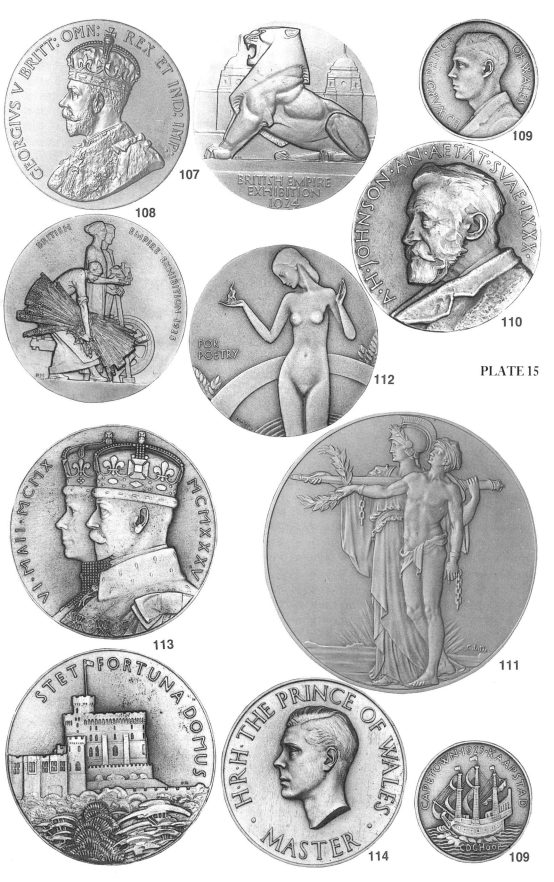

GEORGIVS V BRITT: OMN: REX ET IND: IMP:

107

BRITISH EMPIRE
EXHIBITION
1924

108

EDWARD·PRINCE·OF·WALES

109

BRITISH EMPIRE EXHIBITION 1925

A·H·JOHNSON·AN·AETAT·SVAE·LXXX·

110

FOR
POETRY

112

PLATE 15

VI·MAII·MCMX   MCMXXXV

113

111

STET FORTUNA DOMVS

H·R·H· THE PRINCE OF WALES
· MASTER ·

114

CAPETOWN 1925 KAAPSTAD
C D GH o O P

109

PLATE 16

A particularly interesting composition by C.L. Doman commemorates the tenth anniversary of the Armistice in 1928. It shows the Cenotaph (in London) (*obv.*), and an allegory of Deliverance, with the advance of Great Britain supporting a youthful warrior who offers a wreath to the memory of fallen heroes (*rev.*) (**111**). This stirring medal is unusual in that it was sponsored by the Royal Mint, from which it could be purchased.

In November 1932 the King announced his intention of offering an annual medal for poetry in English. The obverse carried a portrait of the King by Mackennal, and for the reverse the Royal Mint Advisory Committee selected, from a field of ten designs, Edmund Dulac's sensitive and striking illustration of Truth emerging from her well, holding the divine flame of Inspiration (**112**). Dulac, who was paid £113 for the Poetry Medal, is best remembered as an illustrator of children's books and a designer of postage stamps.

In October 1934 Metcalfe was given sittings by George V and Queen Mary for a medal commemorating their silver jubilee. Metcalfe's representation of Windsor Castle symbolizes George V as first monarch of the House of Windsor. The King did not particularly like this idea, preferring something more on the lines of the royal coat of arms and a crown surrounded by shields of the Dominions. The Advisory Committee found that this was not feasible because of the difficulty in including all the shields of the Dominions without causing either confusion or jealousy (PRO Mint 20/1331B). Metcalfe was paid 300 guineas for the medal, which is a definitive statement of the period (**113**), its distinctive formalized design complementing his reverse on the jubilee crown.

The medal was available in sizes of 57 mm and 32 mm, with gold at 40 guineas and 12 guineas, and silver at 15s. 9d. and 1s. 10d. For the first time, the Royal Mint appointed agents (Messrs. Baldwin and Messrs. Spink, London coin and medal dealers) to retail the medals. In January 1935, Spink offered the silver medal to Selfridges, the department store in London, for 18s. and 2s., to retail at 21s. and 2s. 6d. 'We anticipate', they said, 'a very great demand for these Medals, and if you agree with us in this, we would like to suggest your making a very special feature of them'. The response from Selfridges was lukewarm: 'we do not know whether you are suggesting this as a commercial proposition, but the margin of profit is absurd'. Johnson was able to act as mediator, eventually persuading Selfridges and Boots, the chemists, to stock the medal (PRO Mint 20/1332). Private medal-manufacturers were also, of course, making and selling their own versions, as they had done for previous coronations and jubilees. Thomas Fattorini Limited produced a wide variety of medals and related memorabilia for the 1935 jubilee. 'Every boy and girl will want to wear one on the 6th of May' proclaimed their poster, which lists the range of products, including medals with standard portraits, coupled with either an inscription or a coat of arms: prices per

1,000, from £5 10s. to £8 10s. in aluminium, and from £15 10s. to £25 in best quality white metal, according to size. Corporations and committees requiring even larger quantities were invited to submit their orders.

In March 1935 the President of the Royal Numismatic Society, Percy Webb, wrote to the Lord Chamberlain's office saying that the Society wished to strike a centenary medal and that 'in view of His Majesty's gracious patronage of the Society, it is thought that the most appropriate obverse design would be a portrait of The King'. On 18 March 1935, Johnson made it plain 'that permission could not be given to use The King's effigy on their proposed medal, even though it is a Royal Society' (PRO Mint 20/1389). The sovereign's effigy could only be used on medals presented personally.

Thomas Humphrey Paget's origins lie in the British Empire Exhibition, although there is little remarkable about his early work. In 1935, the Honourable Company of Master Mariners wished to institute a medal for award to cadets. They received designs from a number of artists, but the work was given to Paget who produced a portrait of considerable authority. The medal (**114**), which was struck by the Mint, gained the approval of the Prince of Wales and marked the turning point in his career. Paget went on to design the coinage for Edward VIII, prior to his abdication, the portrait based on his Master Mariners' medal, and the definitive coinage portrait of George VI.

Gilbert Bayes had trained at the Royal Academy Schools, and in 1899 won a travelling scholarship. He specialized in reliefs and statuettes, but also produced a number of medals, several for Pinches. In early 1935, Bayes suggested the idea of a medal for the forthcoming launching of the *Queen Mary* to an enthusiastic Johnson, who was aware of a French medal which had recently been struck for the *Normandie*. This medal could be purchased by passengers on board and was, reported Johnson (October 1935), no doubt enviously, 'still selling like hot cakes on every voyage'. Cunard White Star, owners of the *Queen Mary*, accepted the proposal for a medal which, it was hoped, would carry the effigy of Queen Mary herself. However, Buckingham Palace would not permit the use of any royal head. Gilbert Bayes' original design (*see* **fig. 22**) contrasted the *Santa Maria*, Columbus' ship, with the *Queen Mary*, but Cunard's Percy Bates felt that the fate of that ship deemed its use inappropriate. Johnson's proposal of an impressionist view of New York, seen through the Bargate in Southampton, was employed by Bayes for the reverse, and this, coupled with a modified form of his original design, was to constitute the medal (**115**). The precise wording of the Latin inscription had caused some disagreement. Rudyard Kipling, a friend of Percy Bates, proposed 'A Queen Confided me to the Ocean', in Latin 'Regina Me Commisit Pellago'. Johnson, unsure of the accuracy of the translation, consulted three Latin scholars who all preferred 'Maria Regina Mari Me Commisit'.

Fig. 22 Unaccepted design for a *Queen Mary* medal

Percy Bates wrote for further comments to Kipling, who retorted: 'Medal. All right! If your three Latinists think they can improve on Horace (Bk.1: Ode 3: Line 11) don't try to stop 'em. I couldn't so I stole' (PRO Mint 20/ 1396A). In the event, it was the Latinists' opinion which prevailed. Bayes received £100 for his work on the medal, which fully captures the mood of the moment. In all, 3,000 were struck in bronze, each priced at 15s., available from the Royal Mint and on the ship. A handful were struck in gold and examples presented to the King and Queen, the President of the United States and Mrs Roosevelt.

The coronations of Edward VIII (which never took place) and George VI produced a surfeit of privately-manufactured medals, as had previous coronations and jubilees. Two of the less predictable medals anticipating that of Edward VIII were struck in Vienna, in honour of his recent visit. Ludwig Hujer's portrait is rather fanciful and undignified, while that by Johann Joseph Tautenhayn, although hardly flattering, does at least hint at a likeness (**116**). Metcalfe made the official medal for the coronation of George VI in 1937, recalling in the portraits his jubilee medal of George V. The Royal Mint provided manufacturers with obverse portraits of George VI and Queen Elizabeth by Langford Jones, to be used on their privately-made medals. Spink's utilized this not only for a coronation medal, but also for one commemorating the opening of the National Maritime Museum in the same year.

In the autumn of 1937 a landmark conference was held in Paris to consider various aspects of medal-manufacture. The result was the formation of the Fédération Internationale de la Médaille, today commonly referred to as FIDEM. Its principal objectives are the encouragement of public interest in modern medals and their study, and Johnson himself was one of the founder-members. In March 1938 Johnson died quite suddenly. His many initiatives throughout sixteen years at the Royal Mint were largely responsible for its new-found impetus and the raising of standards of medallic art in Britain. Although he had been knighted in the late 1920s, it would have been equally appropriate had he been commemorated by a portrait medal, as his father had been (**110**).

The royal tour to North America by George VI and Queen Elizabeth in 1939 was commemorated by a medal with their conjoined portraits (*obv.*), and a relief map of Canada, delineating the route (*rev.*). The portraits, by P. Metcalfe, had been used on the official 1937 coronation award medal, but remodelled to allow its production on coining presses. The reverse was by the Canadian sculptor and coin-engraver Emmanuel Hahn, and the medal was issued in gold, silver and tombac (an alloy of copper and zinc). Smaller medals, based on this design, were produced at the Royal Canadian Mint, Ottawa, the quantities of which were 250,000 in silver and 500,000 in bronze, corresponding in size to the Imperial half-crown and the Imperial penny, respectively.

John Craig, Johnson's successor, instigated a medal competition in 1939, but his plans were interrupted by the Second World War. There was now little to promote enthusiasm for the medal, with resources being directed towards more pressing needs. Pinches were in fact able to adapt one of their medal presses for gun sights. The Royal Mint was caught up by the effects of war, such as the supplying of military medals; these included the production of over eight million Campaign Stars, much of which had to be contracted out to private firms, as had been done in the past. In 1945 a competition was drawn up by the Mint for a general issue Defence Medal. Competitors included Percy Metcalfe, but it was the rather bland design by Harold Wilson Parker, designer of the 'wren' farthing, which was chosen. Craig steered the administration of the Mint through the Second World War with some finesse, as well as having overseen the introduction of a new cupro-nickel coinage in 1947. However, he does not appear to have imparted the same enthusiasm to good medal design as his predecessor or, at least, to have been aware of its benefits.

The first great national event following the peace of 1945 was the marriage between Princess Elizabeth and Prince Philip of Greece and Denmark in 1947, for which the Mint did not produce a medal. However, one was struck for the royal visit to South Africa in the same year, using Metcalfe's conjoined portraits of George VI and Queen Elizabeth, as on the 1937 coronation award medal (*obv.*), and a royal monogram (*rev.*). One of Metcalfe's last medals was for the Royal Society of Arts, with a portrait of Princess Elizabeth, its president (*obv.*), and a view of the Society's building (*rev.*). It is a strangely dated and uncompromising design and a nostalgic reminder of the pre-war period of medal making (**117**).

Fred Kormis, one of the few medallists making cast medals in this

Fig. 23 Kormis: Laurence Olivier

period, came to London from Frankfurt in the 1930s. Since that time, he produced a large number of cast portrait medals of well-known contemporaries. They include Leslie Hore-Belisha in 1941 (whose legacy as Minister of Transport was the introduction of traffic guides, now known as belisha beacons), Alexander Fleming in 1947, and two of Laurence Olivier (*see* **fig. 23**) in 1949 and again in 1983, one of his last. Kormis' style changed very little over what, for a medallist, was an unusually long working life. Paul Vincze (**118**) was born in Hungary and came to England in 1938. Since the late 1940s, he has produced a large number of medals, struck in low relief, with a matt surface, and in a readily identifiable but somewhat lack-lustre style. They include portraits of John Craig in 1949, Queen Elizabeth II 1953, the sesquicentenary of the Battle of Trafalgar in 1955, Shakespeare's anniversary in 1964 and members of the British Museum's Department of Coins and Medals.

The coronation of Elizabeth II in 1953 was commemorated by a currency crown and an award medal, but not by an official commemorative, thus breaking a 350-year-old tradition, beginning with James I in 1603. The production of commemorative medals was left entirely to the private medal trade, but in order that they be of sufficiently high standard the Royal Mint Advisory Committee agreed to the appointment of a Coronation Medal Panel. The Panel examined and reported upon designs for medals offered for public sale, thirty-seven of which were eventually accepted. Mary Gillick, who produced the first coinage portrait of the Queen, also engraved medals for the Mint, including one for the Royal Commonwealth tour of 1953–4. Paget's obverse portrait of the Queen was supplied to the South African Mint and used on their coronation medals, and he continued making medals for the following twenty years, mostly for organizations.

Post war austerity aside, the Mint was involved with the recovery of silver from coinage in circulation, of which eighty-eight million ounces was needed in order to repay the lend-lease war debt to the United States. In addition, the gentlemen's agreement of 1925, reached between the Mint and private medallists, was casting its shadow. Mint officials were not actively soliciting for medal work, even though, as Johnson had shown, the direction and influence of the Mint and its work were largely in the hands of the Deputy Master. Without the initiative for good medal work coming from the Mint or, for that matter, from any private body, standards were allowed to decline.

A climate was conceived in which the medal flourished during the 1960s, but purely as a medium of investment. Events such as the deaths of Winston Churchill and Albert Schweitzer, and a succession of anniversaries, were commemorated. It was a climate fuelled by changes governing the sale of gold and the low price of precious metals, one in which private medallists marketed medals in 'limited editions', some in a series which the 'collector' would purchase by monthly instalments. One company balloted clients for subjects of popular interest, which would then be commemorated by medals. The prices bore no relationship to their intrinsic worth, but were based solely on rarity and 'investment value'. The art of the medal itself was of little consideration, but lack of taste cannot be held entirely to blame when the choice and the availability of other medals are restricted, as indeed they were. At any rate, the realization that such medals were not the way to riches quelled the interest, but not before vast numbers had been sold.

Harold Glover (119) became Deputy Master of the Mint in 1970. He was keen to revitalize interest in and raise standards of medal-making, and introduced a number of important initiatives, including for the first time the installation of a casting unit. He secured the appointment of a design consultant, Graham Hughes, who in 1973 organized the 'Medals Today' exhibition held at Goldsmiths' Hall, London. This was sponsored by the Worshipful Company of Goldsmiths, with the object of promoting medals back to their original status and, thereby, attracting patrons interested in the medal as an art form. It contained recently-made medals by over forty British artists, most of them used to working in fields other than medals, as well as many made by foreign artists. Among the work shown was that of Malcolm Appleby, who both hand-engraves his dies

PLATE 17

121

120

123

124

122

PLATE 18

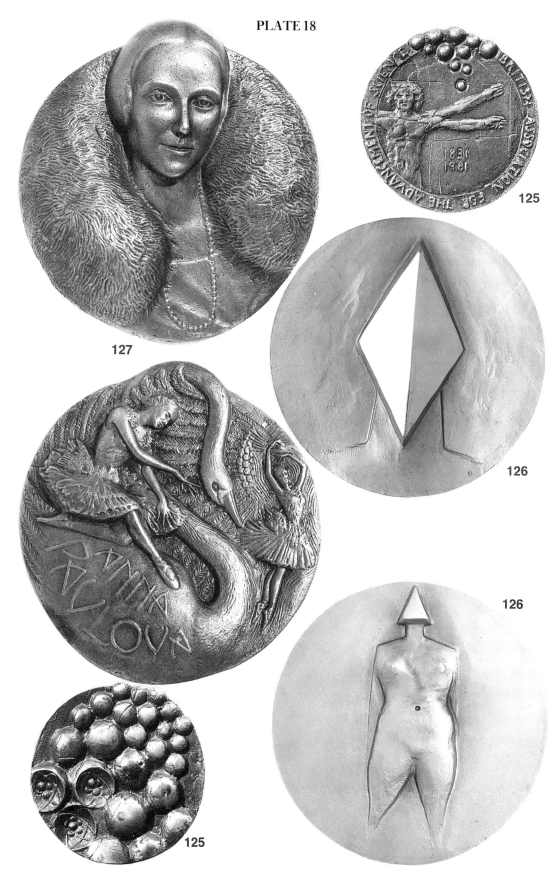

127

125

126

126

125

and hand-strikes his medals, such as that which commemorates the exhibition itself (**120**); Geoffrey Clarke, a sculptor who has worked with glass and metal, exhibited a group of cast medals containing progressive statements on man's destruction of the environment; and Louis Osman, a goldsmith and silversmith, exhibited his Royal Mint Queen's Award Medal (**121**).

In 1974, the Royal Society of Arts, with the initiative and support of Harold Glover, and initially sponsored by B.A. Seaby Limited, introduced a Medals Section into its Design Bursaries Competition. The RSA was well connected with art colleges throughout the country and was therefore in a position to introduce to student artists, particularly sculptors, the art of medal-making. The short-listed medals in the Bursaries Competition were made at the Mint's newly-introduced casting unit, and judged by a jury consisting of representatives of museums, the Mint, practising sculptors and the competition's sponsors.

In the mid 1970s, the Royal Mint completed its move from Tower Hill, London, to Llantrisant in South Wales. An inspired and imaginative proposal was made to utilize the old, now redundant, Mint building at Tower Hill, both as a national museum of coins and medals, as well as an all-purpose numismatic centre. This was another initiative with which Glover was associated, but his move from the Mint to the Stationery Office in 1974 could not have occurred at a less opportune time. Sadly, the project never came to fruition as it would have been of great value to many people, introducing a largely-ignored but integral aspect of our cultural tradition.

Influences of the medal as sculpture were reaching Britain, as seen at the 'Medals Today' exhibition in 1973, and through the FIDEM biennial congresses during the 1970s, held at Cologne 1971 (where Glover was the British representative), Helsinki 1973, Cracow 1975, Budapest 1977 and Lisbon 1979, each an international showcase of the latest medallic work. In Britain, a number of artists were now beginning to respond to the possibilities offered by the medal, a medium to which they were to turn with greater frequency.

Jacqueline Stieger is a sculptor and jeweller who usually casts and patinates her own work. She won the Prix Renouveau de la Médaille in Paris in 1974 for her medal 'Grow Food', and exhibited at the 1975 and 1977 FIDEM congresses. She has produced a variety of medals (**125**) and returned to the theme of food in 1982 with 'Food Furrows' (**122**). Ron Dutton was equally committed to the cast medal in Britain at that time, and is today one of the most prolific medallists of his generation. Like Stieger, he has been concerned less with the portrait, in itself a departure from the medallic tradition, than with landscape and the natural elements. The means by which this is tackled break new ground and represent themes which he has explored and returned to in various ways (**123–4**).

Robert Elderton's medal marking the end of production at the Royal Mint in 1975 was, like his Glover medal which shares a similar reverse (**119**), made at the Mint's casting unit. Elderton, an engraver for the Mint, has introduced a number of imaginative features into his work, which covers a wide range of subject-matter (**127–8**).

In 1979 an exhibition containing several hundred medals, from all periods and from many medal-making schools, was held at the British Museum. In its coverage and approach, 'The Medal, Mirror of History' was a landmark exhibition. It was organized by Mark Jones, a curator at the British Museum, whose complementary catalogue, *The Art of the Medal*, is a fine legacy. The momentum of interest in medals and medal-making was now being maintained and a new generation of artists was coming to fruition, including Lloyd Carter, Annabel Eley, Marian Fountain, Mark Holloway, Cecilia Leete, Jane McAdam and Nicola Moss, several of them Royal Society of Arts Bursary winners.

An energy was now operating on several fronts, including that from a growing number of medal collectors and dealers. In 1977, the idea of a British medal society was conceived by Mark Jones with the collaboration of Ron Dutton, and came to be fully realized in 1982 in the form of the British Art Medal Society. Its principles, of reviving the cast medal and fostering medallic art and history, were and are perfectly in tune with the already-thriving societies on the Continent, such as the Belgian-Dutch Society of Friends of the Medal, which was producing and exhibiting medals before the First World War, and Finland's Guild for Medallic Art, established in 1965. After the encouragement provided by the Royal Society of Arts in the 1750s and subsequently, as well as that of the Society of Medallists in the 1880s, it is only fitting that Britain should have a society concerned exclusively with the subject and its best interests. In many respects, the history of the medal in Britain, of its makers and of its art, seems to be one of false dawns. Why that should be is not altogether clear, although the general observation of George Francis Hill, the distinguished authority on Renaissance medals, that 'a country has the medallists it deserves' (*Medals of the Renaissance*, 1920), has an uncomfortably clear ring of truth about it.

Today, however, things look promising. A large number of artists – jewellers, silversmiths, engravers, and sculptors – are now making medals, all following the conventions of their own craft. Over forty alone have already produced medals for British Art Medal Society, among them Marian Fountain (*see* Contents page), Jacqueline Stieger (**122**), Ron Dutton (**124**), Lynn Chadwick (**126**), Cecilia Leete (**129**), Jane McAdam (**130**), Ronald Searle (**131**), Ian Hamilton Finlay (**132**), Ron Pennell (**133**) and Michael Rizzello (**134**). Original and imaginative in concept, their work looks set to play a part in securing the future of the medal in Britain, and in further expanding its horizons.

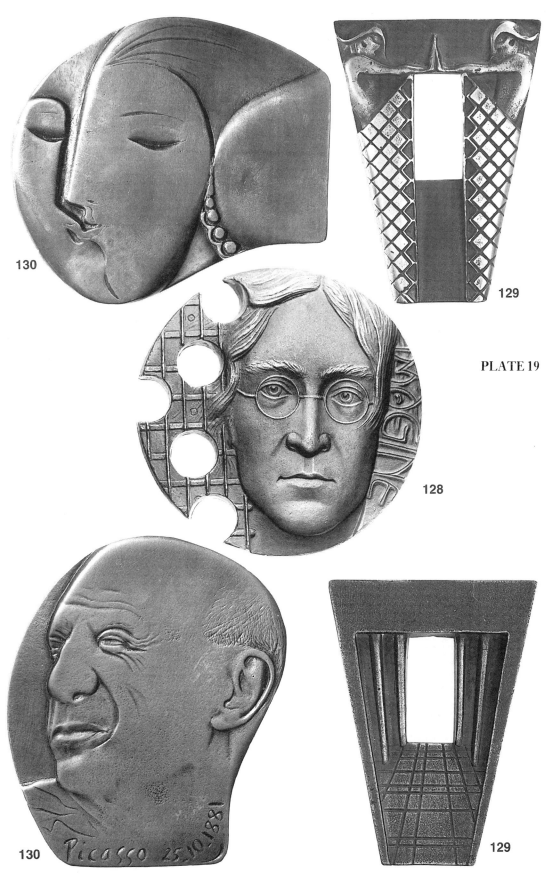

130

129

PLATE 19

128

130   Picasso 25.10.1881

129

PLATE 20

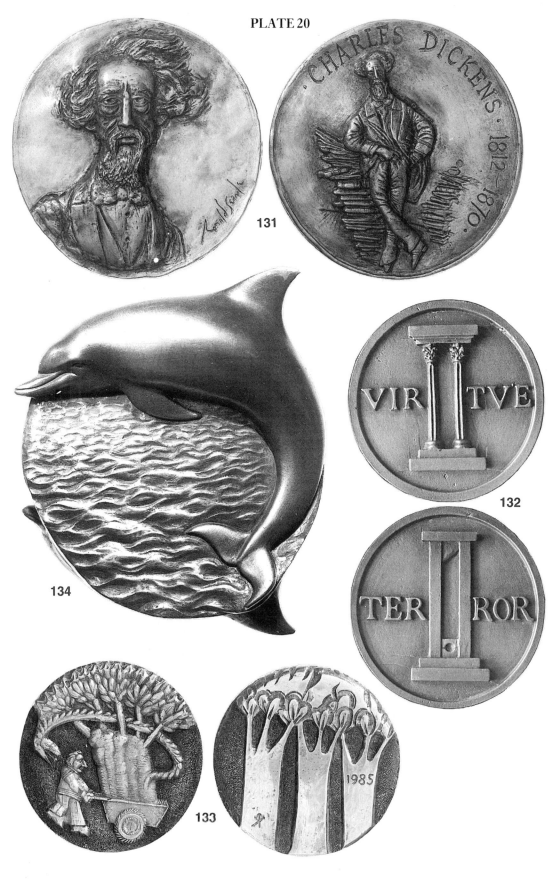

131

132

133

134

Chapter 4

The medal and its subject-matter

Royal Events

Medals relating to royalty include many aspects and have a history going back to the beginning of medal-making in Britain. For coronations and jubilees, the Royal Mint produced both commemorative (*see* Chart, p. 59) and award medals. Their first coronation medal, that of Edward VI in 1547 (**21**), is cast. It is the rarest of the series, and is likely to have been made under the guidance of the Chief Engraver, Henry Basse. Those of James I (**23**) and his queen, Anne of Denmark (**135**), are similar to each other, but probably by different hands. The medal of Anne of which there are minor varieties is the only one to carry an almost-facing portrait, and may not have been struck for the coronation itself.

Medals of Charles I and Charles II commemorate each of their two coronations. Those of Charles I, in London in 1626 and in Edinburgh in 1633 (**28**), are both by N. Briot; the edge of the latter is sometimes lettered, the only one in the series to be so. The first of Charles II, a cast medal (**136**), commemorates his coronation in 1651 at Scone Palace, Perth. Little is known about the manufacture or issue of this rare medal, examples of which occur in a worn state. After the Restoration, the second coronation in 1661 of Charles II in London, is commemorated by T. Simon's medal. It is the first to carry a scene of the coronation, Fame hovering, crown in hand, above the enthroned king (**137**).

The coronation of 1685 is commemorated by single portrait medals of James II (**138**) and Mary of Modena (**139**), both by J. Roettiers. That of William and Mary in 1689 is commemorated by a single medal with conjoined portraits (**140**), also by Roettiers. Anne's coronation medal (**141**) of 1702 and that of George I (**142**) in 1714 were engraved by J. Croker, who also made two medals in 1727 of George II and his queen, Caroline of Brandenburg-Ansbach (**143**). Dual medals were used again, the final time, for the coronation of George III (**144**) and Charlotte of Mecklenburg-Strelitz (**145**) in 1761. Both are by L. Natter and must have presented problems in manufacture, as they have been struck from a number of very similar dies, each with minor varieties.

The medal for George IV's coronation in 1821 is a neo-classical design by B. Pistrucci (**84**). The coronation of William IV in 1831 is commemorated by W. Wyon's medal, which carries a portrait of Adelaide of Saxe-Meiningen on the reverse (**86**). Pistrucci's medal for Victoria's coronation (**146**) in 1838 recalls, both in line and in composition, his George IV medal. The coronation of Edward VII in 1902 is commemorated by G.W. De Saulles' medal, with a portrait of his consort, Queen Alexandra of Denmark, on the reverse (**101**). It was the first to be issued in two sizes, as were medals for the coronations of George V in 1911 by B. Mackennal (**98**), and George VI in 1937 by P. Metcalfe (**147**), again, with their respective consorts on the reverse. The proposed coronation of Edward VIII was not marked by an official commemorative medal, as he had merely acceded to the throne in 1936 and abdicated later in the year. No official medal was struck for the coronation of Queen Elizabeth II in 1953.

For the coronations of James I to Victoria, these medals were distributed during the ceremony as a token of largesse on behalf of the sovereign. The circumstances surrounding this charming tradition varied from one coronation to another, as did the distribution itself, which was carried out by an office such as the Treasurer of the Household, or the Speaker of the House of Commons. Among those receiving gold medals were privy councillors, peers, members of parliament, foreign ambassadors and ministers. Royal servants such as chaplains, physicians and ushers, as well as spectators witnessing the ceremony, received silver medals. One commentary on the coronation of Charles II at Westminster Hall (*A brief narrative of his Majestie's Solemn Coronation*, by Elias Ashmole, London, 1662) records that after homage was paid to the King:

> the Lord High Chancellor went to the South, West and North sides of the stage and proclaimed to the people the King's general pardon . . . And at these three sides at the same time, did the Lord Cornwallis, Treasurer of his Majesty's Household, fling abroad the Medals both of Gold and Silver, prepared for the coronation, as a Princely Donation or Largesse among the People.

At Anne's coronation in 1702, gold medals were given to members of parliament and foreign ambassadors, both of whom would probably have been handed them personally, while the populace received silver medals, distributed by means of scattering. The coronation ceremony for George I took place while Parliament was not in session and no member received a medal. At that of George III, gold medals bearing the effigy of the King were given to peers and privy councillors, while peeresses received gold medals of Queen Charlotte. At the coronation of George IV, apart from a distribution to dignitaries and the populace, silver copies were made of the official medal and given to the Buckinghamshire Yeomanry Coronation Horse, the royal escort; the edges usually engraved B.Y.C.H. Among the gold medals distributed at William IV's coronation were those given to members of parliament, and also occur with an edge inscription.

The scattering of medals often provoked a certain amount of disorder. Newspaper reports of Victoria's coronation, the last at which it took place,

PLATE 21

135

136

137

138

139

140

141

142

143

144

145

146

PLATE 22

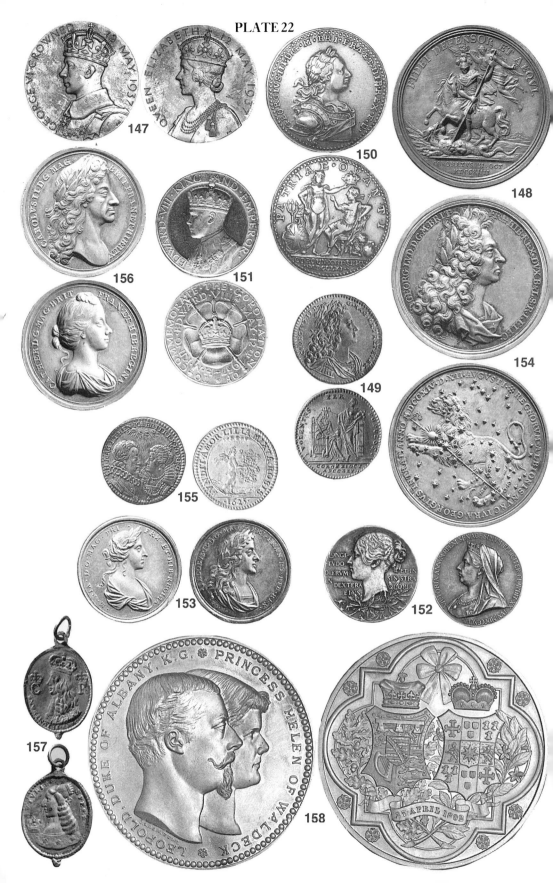

Royal Mint commemorative medals: coronations, jubilees and investitures

CORONATION	Date	Medallist	Diameter	Gold	Silver	Bronze
Edward VI	1547	H. Basse?	62 mm	◊	◊	?
James I	1603	C. Anthony?	29 mm	none	◊	none
Charles I	1626	N. Briot	30 mm	◊	◊	none
Charles I	1633[1]	N. Briot	30 mm	◊	◊	none
Charles II	1651[2]	J. Balfour?	31 mm	◊	◊	none
Charles II	1661	T. Simon	29 mm	◊	◊	none
James II	1685	J. Roettiers	35 mm	200	800	◊
Mary of Modena	1685	J. Roettiers	35 mm	100	400	?
William and Mary	1689	J. Roettiers	35 mm	515	1,200	?
Anne	1702	J. Croker	35 mm	858	1,200	◊
George I	1714	J. Croker	35 mm	330	1,200	◊
George II	1727	J. Croker	35 mm	236	800	◊
Caroline	1727	J. Croker	35 mm	136	400	◊
George III	1761	L. Natter	35 mm	858	800	◊
Charlotte	1761	L. Natter	35 mm	150	400	◊
George IV	1821	B. Pistrucci	35 mm	1,060	800	◊
William IV	1831	W. Wyon	33 mm	1,000	2,000	1,000
Victoria[3]	1838	B. Pistrucci	35 mm	1,369	2,209	1,871
Edward VII	1902	G.W. De Saulles	55 mm	861	7,811	27,456
Edward VII	1902	G.W. De Saulles	31 mm	2,728	102,454	none
George V	1911	B. Mackennal	50 mm	225	2,117	6,253
George V	1911	B. Mackennal	31 mm	719	25,241	none
George VI	1937	P. Metcalfe	57 mm	274	9,051	none
George VI	1937	P. Metcalfe	31 mm	422	87,143	78,078
JUBILEE						
Victoria	1887	J. Boehm and	77 mm	none	2,289	4,257
Victoria	1887	F. Leighton	58 mm	944	◊	none
Victoria	1897	G.W. De Saulles[4]	56 mm	3,725	27,728	41,857
Victoria	1897	G.W. De Saulles[4]	26 mm	19,498	246,270	none
George V	1935	P. Metcalfe	57 mm	100	9,649	none
George V	1935	P. Metcalfe	30 mm	247	167,743	400[5]
Elizabeth II[3]	1977	B. Sindall	57 mm	360	5,000	2,000
Elizabeth II[3]	1977	B. Sindall	44 mm	400	5,000	1,500
INVESTITURE						
Edward	1911	W.G. John	35 mm	129	5,441	◊[5]
Charles	1969	M. Rizzello	58 mm	none	1,525	3,000
Charles	1969	M. Rizzello	45 mm	none	7,500	none
Charles	1969	M. Rizzello	32 mm	none	none	29,000

Notes

◊ made in this metal, but quantity unknown

? possibly made in this metal

[1] coronation in Edinburgh

[2] coronation at Scone Palace, Perth

[3] examples were also struck in platinum

[4] (*obv.*) after W. Wyon; (*rev.*) after T. Brock

[5] not officially issued in this metal

quantities stated are taken from mint records

CORONATION MEDALS, 1902.

Arrangements have been made for the issue of medals by the Royal Mint to commemorate the Coronation of His Majesty King Edward VII.

These medals will be struck in two sizes.

The large medals will be about two-and-a-quarter inches in diameter and be issued in fine gold, fine silver and bronze.

The small medals will measure about one-inch-and-a-quarter in diameter and be issued in fine gold and fine silver only.

The prices will be as follows :—

	£	s.	d.
Large gold (in case)	13	0	0
Small „ „	2	12	6
Large silver „	0	10	0
Small „ (without case)	0	1	0
Bronze (in case)	0	3	0

No issue will be made until *after* the Coronation.

In England, the medals will be obtainable, *on personal application*, at the Head Office of the Bank of England, and at its London Branches in Burlington Gardens and Fleet Street ; also at its Country Branches at Manchester, Birmingham, Liverpool, Bristol, Leeds, Newcastle, Hull, Plymouth and Portsmouth.

In Ireland and in Scotland they will be obtainable, *on personal application*, at the Bank of Ireland, Dublin, and the Bank of Scotland, Edinburgh, and their respective Country Branches.

The Banks will not, however, undertake correspondence in connection with the issue of medals, neither will they be forwarded by post or otherwise.

Persons who desire to obtain medals, but cannot attend at the Banks, must arrange for their Banker, or some friend or Agent, to apply on their behalf.

Applications will be registered as received, and, as far as possible, be dealt with in order of receipt.

ROYAL MINT, LONDON.
May, 1902.

W B & L (c)—56918—2000-5-02

Fig. 24 Royal Mint notice for the 1902 coronation medals

tell of the gentry fighting for medals, a scene quite out of keeping with the dignity of the occasion. The number of people attending the coronation of Edward VII in 1902 was far greater than at previous coronations, and the unseemly scrimmages were now avoided. Another issue of medals was introduced with the coronation of Edward VII. The essential difference was that one was purely commemorative, while the newcomer, of different design, was awarded to a specific person such as an attendant or usher, a member of the Royal Household, or a member of the Services, in recognition of duties performed. These award medals had a suspension loop and ribbon, whereby they could be worn on the chest, alongside any military or civil decorations that had been won.

Mint records provide the numbers of official commemorative medals struck for coronations, as well as those for jubilees and investitures (*see* Chart, p. 59), although they should be treated with some caution. For example, it seems unlikely that the ratio between extant gold and silver medals of George III is as low as the figures would suggest. An account needs to be taken of the medals melted down for their intrinsic value. Official medals were available for purchase by the public from the Royal Mint (*see* **fig. 24**), from banks, as well as through retail jewellers such as Rundell, Bridge and Rundell, and Garrard's. Prices of these medals varied; those of William IV, for example, in gold being £5, silver 10s., and bronze 5s. Discounts would have been given to certain public service employees such as those at the Mint.

Privately-made medals were also produced, the first of which was for the coronation of Charles II in 1661. They comprise at least seven different types (**37**), including small cheaply-made medalets for sale on the streets. Unofficial medals struck for the coronations of James II, Anne, George I (**148**), and subsequent sovereigns occur in a variety of metals. Some, such as that of George II (**149**), are usually of brass, coarse in execution, and imitate the official medals. Various copies of both the George III (**150**) and Charlotte coronation medals were made in brass, bronze and silver, again closely imitating the official issues. Subsequent coronations from that of George IV, with over forty medals, have been commemorated with ever-increasing numbers, including the many struck in anticipation of the coronation of Edward VIII (**151**). The coronation of Edward VII is the first for which local medals were struck by towns or boroughs, where they were often published and retailed by a local jeweller. The obverse sometimes taken from a standard issue portrait, coupled with the town or borough's shield or arms. The majority of these medals are found in white metal or bronze, frequently attached to a ribbon, to be worn during the festivities.

The first of the official Royal Mint jubilee commemorative medals (*see* Chart, p. 59) was struck in 1887 for Victoria's golden jubilee. It carries her bust by J.E. Boehm (*obv.*), and an allegory of the five continents by Frederic, Lord Leighton (*rev.*). For her diamond jubilee in 1897, some desire had been expressed for a special coinage, as had been struck for the golden jubilee. It was, however, considered undesirable for there to be too many different types of coins in circulation, especially as Thomas Brock's 'veiled head' coinage had only been introduced in 1893. A commemorative medal in a reduced size would, it was hoped, go some way towards meeting the wishes of those requiring a special coinage, especially as it carried Brock's coinage portrait. This was coupled with a portrait of Victoria based on William Wyon's 'young head', and the medal was engraved by G.W. De Saulles (**152**).

The precedent of medals in two sizes was observed at the silver jubilee of George V in 1935. The obverse of the smaller size of Metcalfe's medal (**113**) was supplied to the Pretoria Mint by the Royal Mint, and coupled with their own reverse bearing the South African coat of arms. This was one of the many occasions for which the Royal Mint supplied an obverse die to one of the branch mints. The silver jubilee of Queen Elizabeth II in 1977 was commemorated once again with a medal issued in two sizes. The design had been runner-up in the competition for the Queen's jubilee crown. It is an unusual treatment of the sovereign, enthroned and seen facing (*obv.*), with a tudor rose contained within a decorated border (*rev.*), by B. Sindall. Official Royal Mint medals were also struck for the investitures at Caernarvon Castle of Prince Edward and Prince Charles as Princes of Wales in 1911 and 1969 (*see* Chart, p.59).

For the jubilees since 1887, there has also been an official Royal Mint award medal, as there has for coronations since 1902, given to specific people in recognition of their services. The jubilee of George III was the first to be celebrated by unofficial medals. More than twenty-five were struck in 1809 and 1810, anniversaries marking either the start or the completion of his fiftieth year of reign, respectively. The mourning for Prince Albert's death in 1861 disallowed any full celebrations of Victoria's silver jubilee in 1862. Her jubilees of 1887 and 1897, and that of George V in 1935, were each celebrated by numerous private medals. Many, like the coronation medals, were locally-issued, with a standard portrait, coupled with the borough or district's coat of arms, and displayed at the festivities. Victoria's diamond jubilee in 1897 probably saw the largest number of locally-issued medals.

The accessions of Charles II, James II (**153**), George I (**154**), George IV, William IV and Victoria are commemorated on numerous medals, as are royal marriages. Rather commonplace is the small medal made to commemorate the marriage of Charles I and Henrietta Maria, daughter of Henry IV of France in 1625 (**155**), with their facing portraits (*obv.*), and Cupid scattering roses and lilies (*rev.*). The marriage of Charles II and Catherine of Braganza, daughter of John IV of Portugal, took place in 1662. The stability which it promised, coming so soon after the Restoration, is no doubt some reason for its popularity, attested to by the variety of medals (**156**), some of which, the cheaper issues, may have been sold on the streets (**157**). The marriages of Queen Victoria and Prince Albert in 1840, and of the Prince of Wales and Princess Alexandra in 1863, are each commemorated by more than twenty-five medals. The marriages of seven of Victoria's children are commemorated with uniform medals by the Wyons, with the couple's portrait (*obv.*), and their coat of arms (*rev.*) (**158**). Medals recording royal births include those of Prince Charles (II) 1630, Prince James (III) 1688 (**159, 178**), and George (IV) 1762 (**160**). Delightful childhood portraits of seven of Victoria's children are commemorated on a suite of medals by L.C. Wyon (**161**).

The royal visit of George II to Hanover, his homeland and electoral dominions, in 1729, is commemorated with an interesting German medal (**162**) by R. Wahl. One of poor workmanship commemorates the visit of George III and Queen Charlotte to Weymouth in 1805, while others include those to Bath, Cheltenham and Worcester. George IV's visit to Hanover in 1821 and his recent coronation, are together commemorated by C.Voigt's medal: with his portrait (*obv.*), and his equestrian figure (*rev.*). His visits to Ireland in 1821 and Scotland in 1822 are commemorated by more than forty medals, engraved by both English and local medallists. Among the visits which Victoria undertook, and for which

PLATE 23

159

160

161

162

163

164

PLATE 24

165

170

168

175

167

173

166

171

174

176

172

169

medals were struck, are included those to Belgium in 1843, Coburg in 1845, the Channel Islands in 1846, France in 1854, Wolverhampton in 1866, Florence in 1888, Llangollen in 1889 and Ireland in 1900. The Corporation of London's medals commemorating visits include those of Emmanuel II of Sardinia in 1855, Abdul Aziz of Turkey in 1867, George of the Hellenes in 1880, and Edward VII and Queen Alexandra in 1902 (**163**).

As Victoria's representative, the Prince of Wales undertook visits throughout Britain and the Commonwealth. One of the first was to Canada where he attended the opening of the Victoria Bridge, Montreal, in 1860 (**280**). After his marriage to Princess Alexandra of Denmark in 1863, the couple made many visits for which medals were struck, including those to Birmingham, Halifax and Norwich, as well as one to India in 1875–6.

An extensive world tour undertaken in 1900–01 by George (V) and Mary, as the Duke and Duchess of Cornwall, is commemorated on a number of medals, including one of *HMS Orphir*, the ship in which they travelled (**164**). Many are of local interest and record visits to Canada, South Africa and Australia, where the couple officiated at the opening of the first Federal Parliament in 1901. Visits undertaken by Edward (VIII), as Prince of Wales, are also commemorated by medals. One of the first, to the United States in 1919, was marked by the American Numismatic Society with a medal by J. Flanagan. Other visits commemorated include those to Australia in 1920, India in 1921–2, and South Africa (**109**), and Argentina in 1925.

The visit by George VI and Queen Elizabeth to North America in 1939, the first by a reigning British monarch, is commemorated by Royal Mint medals, as is their visit to South Africa in 1947. The visit of Princess Elizabeth and the Duke of Edinburgh to Africa in 1952 is commemorated by a few medals, as is their Commonwealth tour of 1953–4. The Queen's Northern Ireland visit in 1971, on the occasion of its parliament's fiftieth anniversary, is commemorated by a distinctive Royal Mint medal, of which the relief is highly polished and the field is frosted; the bust of the Queen is by T.H. Paget (*obv.*), and Ulster's coat of arms by C. Ironside (*rev.*).

Political and social history

This heading embraces various subjects, in which are bound up those of a satirical and propaganda nature. During the sixteenth and seventeenth centuries, Dutch medallists made considerable use of the medal as a tool of propaganda, often expressing anti-Catholic sentiments. Several late sixteenth-century Dutch medals relate to Britain, such as those for the Armada, one of which depicts the Spanish fleet driven against rocks, the inscription translating as: 'Thou God art great and does wondrous things' (*obv.*), with a scene of the Pope, bishops and kings seated, blindfolded, in discussion, the inscription: 'Oh! the blind minds, the blind hearts of men' (*rev.*) (**165**). Another Dutch medal, dated 1605, refers to the guile of the Jesuits in France, and the discovery of the Gunpowder plot: a snake glides amongst roses and lilies (of England and France), the inscription translating as: 'He who conceals himself is detected' (*obv.*), with the name of Jehovah within a crown of thorns: 'God, the keeper of James I has not slept' (*rev.*) (**166**).

A medal of John Lilburne, a political agitator, celebrates his trial and acquittal of treason on 26 October 1649, after a hearing at the Guildhall lasting three days: it shows his bust and the inscription reads 'saved by the power of the Lord and the integrity of his jury' (*obv.*), with the names of the jurymen (*rev.*) (**167**). A novel feature of this medal, thought to be by T. Simon, are the concentric inscriptions. A portrait medal of Oliver Cromwell, possibly Dutch work *c.* 1655, depicts a seated Britannia, Cromwell kneeling at her feet, undressed, his head on her lap in an attitude of servility. The medal ridicules the French and Spanish ambassadors, each of whom contend to pay their respects, the former insisting (trans.) 'stand back, the honour belongs to the King, my master, Louis the Great' (*rev.*) (**168**).

Catholic–Protestant conflicts and the question of accession to the throne provide the background against which many medals were struck in the latter part of the seventeenth century. One of the more curious intrigues is the Popish Plot of 1678, for which Titus Oates, an imposter, had fabricated a story against the Catholics, alleging that they had conspired to massacre Protestants and assassinate Charles II. As a result of these allegations, to which Oates swore before Edmundbury Godfrey, a Justice of the Peace, a number of Catholics were tried and executed.

A small medal has a bust of Oates (*obv.*), and the King walking by a pond, near to which stands a man with a gun (*rev.*). Another medal has the 'janiformed' head of a Jesuit and a monk (*obv.*), with a cluster of five faces, probably representing the plot's detectors, Lord Clifford, Lord Ashley, the Duke of Buckingham, Lord Arlington and the Duke of Lauderdale, commonly known by the acronym of Cabal (*rev.*) (**169**), by G. Bower. Several medals by Bower commemorate Godfrey, who had been found dead under mysterious circumstances. A common obverse portrays him being strangled with his own cravat (**170**), a scene coupled with several reverses. On one, heads of the pope and devil are joined at the neck to form one face, of which a similar image is produced when inverted (**171**), one widely used on European sixteenth and seventeenth-century medals. Another medal, probably also by Bower, depicts Godfrey walking, having been strangled with his cravat (*obv.*) (**172**), and St Denis walking, head in hand, after his martyrdom (*rev.*).

The Rye House plot of 1683 was a conspiracy to murder the King and his brother, James, Duke of York, next in line to the throne. It was hatched in order to secure the succession of the Protestant James, Duke of Monmouth, the natural son of Charles II and his mistress, Lucy Walters. A medal by Bower depicts Charles II, as Hercules, warding off a Hydra, whose heads are those of the conspirators (*obv.*), with a shepherd watching over his flock in a vale where two wolves (Lord William Russell and Algernon Sidney, illegally convicted and executed) are hanging on a gibbet (*rev.*) (**173**).

On the death of Charles II in 1685, the Duke of Monmouth claimed the right to succession in place of his Catholic uncle James II, and mounted a rebellion which was ruthlessly crushed at the battle of Sedgemoor in Somerset. Several portrait medals of Monmouth ridicule the futility of his attempt, such as one by Bower, which shows the Duke attempting to scale a column, upon which are three crowns (**174**). On another, he is depicted as a Roman warrior, trying to prize open a lion's mouth (**175**). His actual fate is also recorded. One medal, probably by J. Smeltzing, has his bust (*obv.*), while his head lies on the ground spouting blood (*rev.*). On another, by R. Arondeaux, the bust of James II rests on sceptres of State (*obv.*), while Justice, her scales tipped in favour of the Crown rather than weapons of treason, stands between the decapitated bodies of Monmouth and his co-conspirator, Archibald, Duke of Argyll (*rev.*) (**176**).

James II himself was the subject of several satirical medals, a period which saw Dutch medallic propaganda at its most prolific. In 1688, the meeting of Suleyman III of Turkey, Mezzo Morto of Algiers, Louis XIV and James II confirmed the Anti-Christian Confederacy. It is commemorated by a medal, with the protagonists swearing an oath of allegiance (*obv.*), while an imp, wearing a Jesuit's cap and brandishing a sword and thunder, hovers above three lilies (*rev.*) (**177**), by J. Smeltzing. The birth in 1688 of James II's son, Prince James, the 'Old Pretender', is recalled by several medals (**159, 178**). On one, Truth stands against a cupboard door which opens to reveal a Jesuit supporting the infant Prince, crowning himself and being threatened with a puff of wind; a fleet approaches, beyond. The inscription, translated, reads 'James Francis Edward 20 June 1688, supposititious', suggesting that the claim that there was now an heir to the crown was a spurious one. The medal's outer inscription foretells that 'heirs will not be wanting' (*obv.*), with a Trojan Horse (*rev.*), by J. Smeltzing. James II's flight to Ireland in 1689 is recalled on Smeltzing's medals, the common obverse to which carries the bust of James II, his hair tied up in a hair-net in readiness to flee, with the telling inscription 'Jacobus II Britan: Rex Fugitiv' (**179**). It occurs with different reverses: on one, a large oak lies broken (**179**); on another, lightning shatters a column;

and again, this time on a medal commemorating his flight from Ireland in 1690, a winged stag takes fright.

The destruction of Catholic chapels in London, following the accession of William and Mary in 1689, is commemorated on a medal with their conjoined portraits (*obv.*), and chapels burning in a square (*rev.*), by G. Bower. Another, by P.H. Müller, records the stability following the coronation, with their conjoined busts (*obv.*), and Britannia, who is seated beneath orange and rose trees and tramples upon anarchy and tyranny. The inscription (trans.), 'Oranges grow upon flower-bearing rose trees – the security of Britain restored' (*rev.*) (**180**).

In 1696, Sir George Barclay, an ardent Jacobite, hatched a plot against William III in order to restore James II. It is commemorated on a medal with the conjoined busts of Louis XIV and James II (*obv.*), with the two displaying a purse of 100,000 pistoles, to be used as bribery, with armed conspirators beyond (*rev.*). Many Jacobite medals from the 1690s onwards refer to their fortunes (**59**), and in particular those of Prince James, which keep alive the hope that he would become king as James III.

Both English (**52**) and Continental medals commemorate the Peace of Utrecht in 1714. A German version graphically ridicules its conclusion by the English, French and Dutch, who are depicted as three partially undressed men, defecating together beneath a wall; remarks between them indicate common agreement (*obv.*), while they are now seen throwing the contents of their piles at each other (*rev.*) (**181**). Christian Wermuth, the German satirical medallist, may be responsible for this medal, as he might a number ridiculing John Law, a Scottish financier, who started a private bank in France. In 1717, Law floated his Mississippi Scheme but it collapsed in 1720, plunging thousands of families into financial ruin. Some thirty medals poke fun at Law, whose notoriety was such that he left France, and ridicule the French for having placed confidence in such a rascal. On one, Law issues his share certificates from a pair of bellows, the inscription (trans.) inquiring, 'Who in his desire for money will allow himself to be led by the wind' (*obv.*), with Aesop's dog crossing a stream, into which he drops a bone in order to pick up another, that seen in his own reflection (*rev.*) (**182**). On another medal, the sails of a windmill, driven by blasts of air, effortlessly spew jewels, stock certificates and banknotes.

The marriage between Prince James, the 'Old Pretender', and Princess Maria Clementina of Poland, was opposed by George I. Maria Clementina, on her way to Rome to marry James, was arrested and confined to Innsbruck Castle. A medal by O. Hamerani commemorates her escape to Bologna, in 1719, where she was married to James by proxy: with the bust of Maria Clementina (*obv.*), and a hurriedly departing carriage (*rev.*).

Sir Robert Walpole's Excise Bill, first introduced in 1733, provided the means to charge duty on foreign goods such as wine and tobacco. It was

PLATE 25

PLATE 26

very unpopular and eventually led to his defeat, as recalled on a medal with Walpole, leash around neck, being led by the Devil towards the mouth of a fantastic beast and captioned 'make room for Sir Robert' (*obv.*), with the Duke of Argyll, whose removal from office by George II was made on the suggestion of Walpole (*rev.*) (**183**). Another medal commemorates Walpole's defeat and resignation in 1742: his seated figure on a balcony, with the inscription 'I am kicked out of doors' (*obv.*), and a pole (of a traitor) on a wall, a pun on his name (*rev.*) (**184**).

Several medals commemorate John Wilkes, the political reformer and editor of *The North Briton* newspaper, of which an issue (No. 45) in 1768 charged George III with falsehood. Wilkes was prosecuted for libel, but managed to obtain a verdict against the government, with damages for illegal arrest. He was twice expelled from the House of Commons and re-elected as an M.P., and became the idol of mobs, who rioted for 'Wilkes and Liberty', a slogan carried on some of the medals, as is the caption 'No. 45' (**185**).

George Whitefield and John Wesley, the founding fathers of Methodism, are both commemorated by several portrait medals. Those of Whitefield, struck on his death in 1770, include one with a cherub seated upon a funerary urn (*rev.*), by T. Pingo. Several medals of John Wesley and, to a lesser extent, his brother Charles, commemorate Methodist meetings in the 1830s and the centenary of Wesleyan Methodism in 1839. The London Missionary Society, Baptist Missionary Society and Church Missionary Society are all commemorated on medals. The earliest commemorates the London Missionary Society, and the sailing in 1796 of the ship *Duff*, which is depicted (*obv.*), to carry 'missionaries to the South Seas for the conversion of the heathens' (*rev.*).

The curious circumstances surrounding 'Madame' (Charles Geneviève Timotheé De Beaumont) D'Éon, a French transvestite and ambassador living in London, are recalled by an interesting medal of 1777 (**186**); although exactly why it was made and by whom is something of a mystery. In the same year, a civil court action had been fought by two men in respect of a wager concerning D'Éon's gender, a subject which had prompted financial speculation, but one only satisfactorily resolved on his death in 1810. Perhaps coincidentally, the Earl of Mansfield, the presiding judge in the D'Éon affair, appears on a medal by J. Kirk struck in the same year (*obv.*), with Justice holding scales on which are balanced a scroll, and a crown and sceptre (*rev.*).

Several medals recall republican sympathies, prevalent at the time of the French Revolution. One dated 1793, of Thomas Paine (*obv.*), has an embodiment of the 'Mountain in Labour' (*rev.*). Paine was the author of *The Rights of Man*, in which he advocated the overthrow of the English monarchy and defended measures taken in revolutionary France, to where he fled in 1792, after having been tried and convicted of treason.

The trial for treason and acquittal in 1794 of Thomas Hardy (founder of the London Corresponding Society, which espoused Parliamentary reform), John Thelwall and John Horne Tooke is recorded by several medals: one has their portraits (*obv.*), and those of their defending counsel, together with details of the jurors (*rev.*).

Two interesting medals dated 1795, both by W. Whitley, refer to France in quite different ways. Lord Stanhope, the politician and scientist, was chairman of the Revolution Society. In 1794–5 he introduced motions against interference in French affairs over which, as stated on a portrait medal, he was in 'the minority of one'. Whitley's other medal extols the virtues of the monarchy: a scene of blissful family life is endorsed, above, by the imperial crown, the inscription 'God save the king the land we live in and may those who don't like it leave it' (*obv.*), a standing figure of a decapitated French aristocrat points to his head on the ground, beyond stands an imp; the inscription, separated by a band decorated with human heads, advises 'abhor evil cling to that which is good / a philosophical cure for all evils. Licentious liberty is destruction' (*rev.*) (**187**).

A number of clubs and associations were established in the eighteenth and nineteenth centuries, many of a political or quasi-political complexion, for which medals were issued. The 'Glorious Revolution' of 1688 and Protestant ascendancy of William III are recalled on several medals, such as that of the Edinburgh Revolution Club, whose medal, inexplicably dated 1753, has a standing figure of William III (*obv.*), and an inscription commemorating the accession of William and Mary (*rev.*). Orange association and Williamite clubs are commemorated by more than twenty medals, mostly made in the 1790s and thereafter. W. Mossop's medal is typical, with a bust of William III and 'The Glorious and Immortal Memory 1690' (*obv.*), and the Royal Arms and 'King & Constitution' (*rev.*). For the other side, Jacobite clubs were formed to keep alive the Stuart cause, and often operated under a veil of secrecy. A medal dated 1750, and probably by T. Pingo, appears to have been struck at the expense of one such society which met in London. Commonly referred to as the 'Oak Medal', it has a bust of Prince Charles, the 'Young Pretender' (*obv.*), and a leafless oak tree, from which sprouts a flourishing sapling (*rev.*).

The lighter side to life at the time was also celebrated on a number of medals. The Beggars' Benison Club was established in the eighteenth century at Anstruther, Scotland, for frivolities and pleasures of various kinds. It is recorded on at least four medals, mostly struck in the early nineteenth century. They commonly depict the naked figures of Adam and Eve, and the inscription 'Be fruitful and multiply' (*obv.*); on one, a man stands adjacent to a partially nude reclining woman with the inscription 'lose no opportunity' (*rev.*) (**188**). The Catch Club, founded in 1762, also devoted to entertainment, but of a vocal kind, is recalled on a medal by T. Pingo, with two figures playing a lyre and holding a cup, with the inscription 'Let's drink and let's sing together' (*obv.*), and a wreath (*rev.*). Examples were presented to members for the composition or performance of catches and glees at their dinners in London.

The original London Pitt Club was founded in 1793, to counteract the principles of French republicanism and promote those of William Pitt, on whose birthday anniversary it convened. In 1808, two years after Pitt's death, the London Club was revived and a members' badge instituted, consisting of a white glass 'cameo' bust of Pitt, set against a black background on an oval badge decorated with a wreath (**189**). Examples in gilt silver could be purchased by members for £1 16s 6d; those in gold were available to founder members, or to those who had given special services. Rules of the London Club required that 'each member shall wear . . . the Pitt Medal tied on his left breast with a garter blue ribbon' ('Pitt Club Medals', by S.A. Garnett, *BNJ* 2nd series, 1927–28, vol. IX, pp. 213–18). By the time of its dissolution in 1849, the London Pitt Club had elected over 1,700 members. Of the other forty-five or more Pitt clubs throughout Britain, more than fourteen issued their own medals, including those in Birmingham 1814, Rochdale 1813, Stirling 1814, Suffolk 1821 (**190**) and Wolverhampton 1813. Each has a bust of Pitt (*obv.*), usually with an inscription in a wreath (*rev.*); that of Manchester 1813 has a standard bust of Pitt (*obv.*), but with an allegory of Pitt rousing the Genius of Great Britain to resist the demons of anarchy (*rev.*), by T. Wyon Jr.

The success of William Wilberforce in securing the bill for the abolition of the slave trade in 1807 is commemorated on a portrait medal by T. Webb entitling him 'The Friend of Africa' (*obv.*), while the figure of Victory hovers above that of Britannia seated upon a dais inscribed 'I have heard their cry' (*rev.*) (**191**). Several medals were struck for electoral purposes, such as those by Thomason for use by candidates (*see* **fig. 13**), or by the candidate in gratitude to the electorate. A portrait medal of Henry Brougham carries a tribute 'to the patriotic incorruptible and unbought freeholders of the county of Westmoreland IV July MDCCCXVIII' (*rev.*), by G. Mills.

When the price of tickets at Covent Garden Theatre was increased in 1809 riots broke out among Londoners. In an effort to assuage the unrest, John Philip Kemble, actor-manager and owner of the theatre, allowed free admission to boxers, a number of whom were Jews. He thought that this measure would be popular, in view of the esteem in which boxers were held, but it backfired, producing an isolated streak of anti-semitism. The episode is recalled by a medal depicting Kemble as Shylock, with the inscription 'this is the Jew which Shakespeare drew' / 'avrice and titles lust tis a nation's shame' (*obv.*), and another inscription 'the dramas laws, the dramas patrons give, and he who lives to please, should please to live' (*rev.*) (**192**).

Sir Francis Burdett M.P., opposed the war with Napoleonic France and urged parliamentary and prison reform. He was himself imprisoned in 1810 for objecting to the arrest of people merely on the grounds of having organized a political meeting, and is commemorated by a portrait medal (*obv.*), and titled 'The intrepid champion of freedom, the enlightened advocate of the rights and liberties of the people' (*rev.*). An interesting medal dated 1810 recalls Joseph Hanson, the industrial reformer, with his bust (*obv.*), and a loom, spinning wheel and printing machine (*rev.*) **(193)**, by T. Wyon Sr 36,000 people had each contributed one penny towards a fine which, together with a term of imprisonment, had been imposed on Hanson, the 'Weaver's Friend', for his actions on behalf of the Luddites, for whom he campaigned for a minimum wage. An unusual medal recalls the bloody conflict at St Peter's Fields, Manchester in 1819, following speeches and demonstrations against working conditions of the labouring classes. The medal shows a troop of cavalry cutting down men, women and children (*obv.*), the inscription reading 'the wicked have drawn out the sword, they have cut down the poor and needy' (*rev.*) **(194)**. With the victory at Waterloo a fresh memory, the event came to be known as the 'Peterloo Massacre'.

The various events and figures in Ireland's chequered history are also commemorated by a number of medals. One of Ireland's greatest political champions was Daniel O'Connell, whose soubriquet 'The Liberator' is found on a few of the twenty-five or more medals commemorating his career **(195)**. These include his election in 1828 as Member of Parliament for County Clare, the seat which he refused to take up until Wellington and Peel, forced by public opinion, carried through the Bill of Emancipation in 1829, removing Catholic disabilities and thereby allowing them to swear their own Parliamentary oath. Several medals commemorate Charles Stuart Parnell, who united the Fenians and the Irish Land League in a fight for home rule. In 1880 a dispute between Charles Cunningham Boycott, an Irish land agent, and tenants who refused to pay rent or work for him, resulted in agitation by the Land League. A medal by J. Woodhouse was presented 'In honour of the loyal & brave Ulstermen' to the volunteers who gathered in the crops, which the farm labourers would not do. (Incidentally, Boycott's name is now synonymous with a term of exclusion). Theobald Wolfe Tone (1763–98), leader of the United Irishmen, promoted the landing of a French force for the invasion of Ireland in 1798; he was captured and tried for treason but 'escaped' execution by committing suicide. A portrait medal was struck on the centenary, with an Irish harp and the inscription 'who fears to speak of .98' (*rev.*). The shadow of romance also cast itself over Robert Emmet, the United Irishman and rebel, whose attempt to seize Dublin Castle was thwarted, resulting in his trial for treason and subsequent hanging. In 1903 the Emmet Centenary Committee in Australia struck a portrait medal, 'to perpetuate the memory of Ireland's noblest patriot and martyr' (*rev.*).

A large number of medals commemorate the passing of the Reform Bill (**196**) in 1832, and the Corn Laws of 1846. The final passing of the act abolishing slavery throughout the British Colonies (**197**) in 1834, and that for the abolition of negro apprenticeship in 1838, are also commemorated by medals. The establishment of temperance societies in the 1830s and 40s is widely commemorated, with more than twenty medals for those in Ireland. Several portray 'Father' Theobald Mathew, an Irish priest and orator, who was instrumental in their formation (*see* **fig. 17**). The Order of Rechabites, the Total Abstinence Society, the Independent Order of Good Templars and the British and Foreign Temperance Society are among those for which medals were struck in the nineteenth century, many of whose inscriptions warn against the demon drink 'for all except medicinal purposes'.

The return of twelve Conservative members for The Wrekin (Shropshire) in 1841 is commemorated with a medal by T. Halliday: in the centre appear a sword, sceptre and crown upon a cushion, and a ribbon inscribed 'God Save the Queen', while around is a wreath inscribed with the names of the twelve (*obv.*), and a view of The Wrekin (*rev.*). Largely due to Lord John Russell's efforts on behalf of Lionel de Rothschild, the bill for the removal of Jewish disabilities was finally passed in 1858, having successfully gone through the House of Commons on nine previous occasions, to be rejected each time by the Lords. An interesting medal published in 1848 has Russell's bust (*obv.*), with an allegory of a female suckling two infants, the inscription 'have we not all one father, have not one God created us' (*rev.*) (**198**), by Allen and Moore.

The trial in 1874 of the 'Tichborne Claimant' held the record as the longest in English legal history, and recalls a bizarre chain of events, the summary of which concerns Arthur Orton, a butcher, who in 1852 emigrated from England to Australia. In 1866, he returned at the invitation of Lady Tichborne, whom he had deceived into believing him to be her long-lost son and heir (who in actual fact had been missing at sea since 1854). Orton was prosecuted for deception and perjury in two trials lasting 102 and 188 days. One medal carries a bust of Orton (*obv.*), with a bust of a child and a legend 'The alleged rightful heir aged five years' (*rev.*).

Several portrait medals commemorate William Gladstone (**199**), one of the earliest of which records his candidature for South-West Lancashire in 1868. Benjamin Disraeli was also commemorated by medals, almost all of which were struck on his death in 1881 (**200**). Joseph Chamberlain's first election as Member of Parliament for Birmingham in 1876 is recorded on medals, as is his completion of thirty years' service (**201**). His diplomatic mission to South Africa in 1903, the first by a Secretary of State to an overseas colony, is recalled on a medal by J. Fray, his bust with the familiar monocle (*obv.*), and the figure of Peace, her arms out-stretched, the inscription 'I go to South Africa with the most earnest desire to bring together the people into one great African nation under the British flag' (*rev.*).

A medal for the premiership of Lloyd George (**202**) in 1917, by F. Bowcher, is one of few British political medals of the First World War period. Several of the numerous German satirical medals relate to Britain, and provide, paradoxically, the only medallic record of contemporary figures such as Lords Curzon, Fisher and Northcliffe, Sir Edward Grey and Winston Churchill. They are blunt, and sometimes vicious, in their caricatures, the medallic equivalent of the newspapers' political cartoons. It is, for example, no surprise to find a medal of the Irish traitor, Roger Casement who, it is claimed, was tried and executed under an archaic English statute: a manacled figure is strangled from behind (*obv.*), while a book dated 1351 stands upon a spiked chair covered with cobwebs, the inscription (trans.) 'the dead hand of Edward III is tying the rope around Ireland, August 3 1916' (*rev.*) (**203**). It is by Karl Goetz, one of the most prolific exponents of the genre. On Goetz's medal of Lord Northcliffe, the newspaper proprietor (*obv.*), the devil is shown seated on a burning globe, the fire for which is fuelled by title pages of Northcliffe's newspapers, the inscription (trans.) 'the moulder of English public opinion 1914' (*rev.*).

One of the most notorious and still disputed incidents of the First World War is the sinking of the *Lusitania*, with the loss of almost 1,200 lives, torpedoed by the Germans, who claimed it was carrying ammunition. Three days later, on 10 May 1915, the event was being acclaimed in German newspapers, the *Kölnische Volkszeitung* announcing it as an important victory (trans.) 'with joyful pride we contemplate this latest deed of our navy'. The incident is commemorated on a medal by Goetz with a skeleton figure of Death selling tickets to passengers, one of whom reads a newspaper inscribed (trans.) 'submarine danger', while the German ambassador raises a warning finger, the inscription (trans.) 'business first' (*obv.*), with the *Lusitania* depicted as a sinking warship (*rev.*). A number of copies of this medal were made, including an English version, sold to raise funds for war charities. It was issued in a cardboard box with a label on its lid depicting the ship, together with a poster decrying the act as one committed against an unarmed civilian-carrying ship.

The background details to a group of innocent-looking medals exposes their use as political propaganda. In 1926, the British Empire Union, an organization of unbridled nationalism (motto: 'Britain for the British'), issued privately-struck medals in large quantities, with a portrait of the Prince of Wales (*obv.*) and an antique galley seen through the archway of a decorative stone bridge (*rev.*). They were to be given to school children throughout the Colonies on Empire Day, 24 May, and worn with a red, white and blue ribbon.

In 1927 the British Empire Union approached the Royal Mint for a quote, and were surprised to find them marginally cheaper than the company (Pinches?) which had struck their first issue. The Mint were well aware of this potentially lucrative business and, as further inducement, made clear that no charge would be made for the designs. They secured the contract and their medal carried Metcalfe's portrait of the Prince of Wales (*obv.*), and Paget's seated figure representing the Mother Country, after a design by F. Derwent Wood, which originally had been intended for a crown (*rev.*) (**204**). By the end of 1928, and after more than 40,000 medals had been supplied, the Union requested a new reverse, one which would appeal more to children and 'fire them with enthusiasm to emulate the deeds of their forefathers'. Six artists submitted designs and that by C.L. Doman was chosen: an allegory of Mother Country encouraging two children at her side to go forth and perform great deeds (**205**).

However, the distribution of medals bearing an effigy of the Prince of Wales was beginning to raise some eyebrows, and a Parliamentary question (13 June 1928) inquired 'whether a propaganda organization could get their medals struck at the Royal Mint' (PRO Mint 20/1077). Furthermore, a letter (2 January 1929) from the Liberal Party to the Deputy Master complained that the medals were being distributed by a local Conservative organization. On 18 January 1929, R.A. Johnson wrote to the British Empire Union:

> If you could have pointed to a printed circular or catalogue in which you stated that 'these medals could not be issued to Political Organizations, and must not be used in connection with the activities of any political organization' that would have definitely clinched the matter, and we should have no more trouble ... The Mint cannot be held responsible. If there is no such published statement by the B.E.U. I am quite certain that we should very soon find ourselves instructed by Parliament to refuse to supply these medals to you at all. Remember that there is nothing which Liberals resent so much – or, for that matter, all but the extremists in the Labour Party – than the suggestion that the British Empire is the monopoly of the Tory Party (PRO Mint 20/1078).

In March 1929, the Union received a letter from Warren Fisher at the Treasury, indicating that the Prime Minister felt:

> bound to take exception to the reproduction on a document containing phrases lending themselves to a politically controversial interpretation of a medal bearing the effigy of H.R.H. The Prince of Wales and struck

PLATE 27

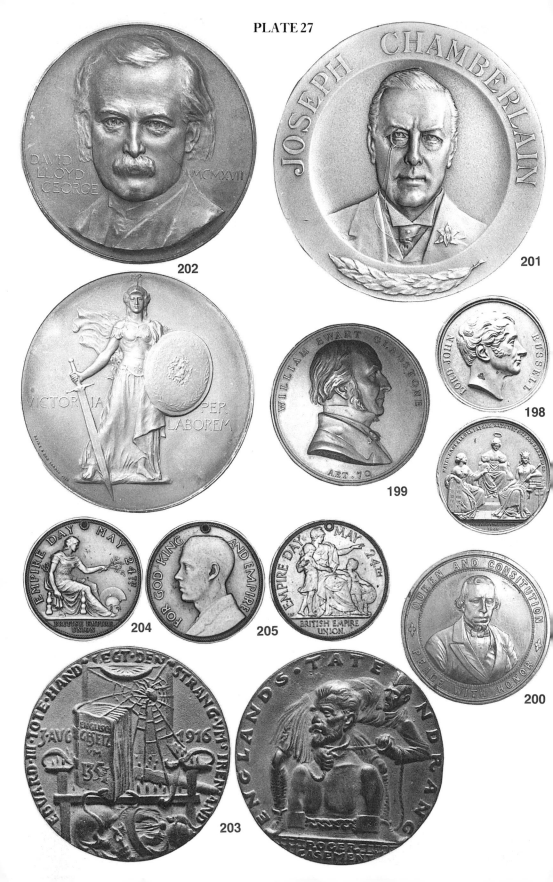

202

201

198

199

204

205

200

203

PLATE 28

at the Royal Mint. Mr. Baldwin, therefore, cannot permit the issue of any further supplies of this medal to your association unless the pamphlet in its present form is withdrawn and suitably emended (PRO Mint 20/1078).

By early 1931, when the Mint had struck more than 75,000 medals, a letter (10 March 1931) from the Treasury considered that 'in view of the questions raised . . . it would be well to leave this particular order to private contractors in future' (PRO Mint 20/1168).

Neville Chamberlain's return from the Munich four-power conference in 1938 was commemorated by several portrait medals. One by L.E. Pinches, heralding his arrival in England, has an olive-branch in the centre and the inscription 'out of the nettle danger he has plucked the flower safety'.

Military and naval history

The first British campaigns commemorated on medals date to the end of the sixteenth century, although only a small number of medals were made in England at this time, all of which are cast. They commemorate the Armada in 1588 and possibly served as naval rewards: one carries a portrait of Elizabeth I (*obv.*), while a bay tree remains untouched by lightning (*rev.*). Most of the medals from this period, however, are of Dutch origin, several of which also commemorate the Armada (**165**): one depicts a large fleet, dispersed and wrecked (*obv.*), and the Protestant Church standing firmly on a rock (*rev.*). The subsequent actions against the Spanish in the 1590s are also recorded on Dutch medals, such as for the invasion defeated in 1696 (**206**), and the battles at Turnhout in 1597 (**207**), Nieuport in 1600 and Rheinberg and Ostend in 1601, many with a battle scene. A medal of 1602 commemorating the capture of Grave by Prince Maurice of Orange and the defeat of Spanish naval squadrons at Goodwin Sands, has an overhead view of Grave, its landscape and rivers identified (*obv.*), and scenes of both a cavalry and a naval engagement (*rev.*).

The English Civil War is recorded on several oval cast portrait medals, including a number by T. Rawlins of the Parliamentary commanders, the earls of Essex (**208**) and Manchester, General Fairfax (**209**) and Sir William Waller (**210**); one of Sir Richard Browne (*obv.*), has his armorial shield and the inscription 'For King and Parliament 1644' (*rev.*). Many of these medals have a wreath border and suspension loop.

The naval action against Holland in 1665, fought off the Lowestoft coast, arose from skirmishes between Dutch and English merchants trading in each others' waters. It is commemorated with two medals by J. Roettiers, which may have served as naval rewards. One has a bust of

Charles II (*obv.*), and a standing figure of the King as a Roman general viewing the engagement (*rev.*) (**43**). The King's brother, the Duke of York, appears on the other, a very fine medal, where he is styled Lord High Admiral of England (*obv.*), with a naval engagement (*rev.*) (**44**). Another medal, the last by T. Simon, also celebrates this victory and confirms Charles II's 'dominion of the seas': with a richly decorated bust of the King (*obv.*) who, holding a trident, is seated in a marine chariot drawn across the waters by sea-horses, and the inscription (trans.) 'the sea too shall obey' (*rev.*) (**41**).

The flight of James II and the accession of his son-in-law William of Orange as William III in 1689 were followed by several battles in Ireland, including those at Londonderry in 1689, the Boyne in 1690, and Aughrim, Athlone and Sligo in 1691. Two interesting medals commemorate the Boyne: one, by J. Luder, has a bust of William III (*obv.*), and the equestrian figure of William pursuing James II and the French commander, the Duc de Lauzun (*rev.*); the other, by P.H. Müller, has a bust of Marshal Schomberg, a German soldier of fortune who was killed at the Boyne (*obv.*), with Schomberg as Hercules and shields of his campaigns (*rev.*). A number of medals were also struck for the pacification of Ireland in 1691 (**211**). The great naval battle in 1692 against France at La Hogue is commemorated by more than thirty English and Continental medals (**212**). One, with the conjoined busts of William and Mary (*obv.*), depicts the French ship *Le Soleil Royal* in flames (*rev.*), probably by J. Roettiers. Subsequent battles at Namur and Steinkirk in the same year, and actions at Havre and Huy in 1694 and again at Namur in 1695, are commemorated by medals.

The reign of Queen Anne saw a similarly large number of medals issued. The capture of French and Spanish fleets by England and Holland at Vigo Bay in 1702 is commemorated on at least eight English, Dutch, French and German (**213**) medals. One of the most common has a crowned bust of Anne (*obv.*), and a view of Vigo harbour in which can be seen burning ships (*rev.*), by J. Croker. Other actions for which several medals were made include Gibraltar in 1704, Barcelona in 1705–06, Lille in 1708, Malplaquet in 1709 (**51**) and Almenara in 1710. Many of these battles were fought under the commands of the Duke of Marlborough and Prince Eugène of Savoy, both of whom are commemorated (**214**). For the Battle of Blenheim in 1704, more than twelve medals were struck: one with the armoured busts of the two commanders facing each other (*obv.*), and a panoramic view of the battle (*rev.*), by M. Smeltzing.

Jacobite attempts to invade Britain in 1708 are recorded on several medals (**215**), as are their actions in 1715 at the battle of Dunblain (Sheriffmuir) and the capture of Preston, each with the bust of George I (*obv.*), with Victory hotly pursuing fleeing cavalry on one (**53**), and two captives chained to a pedestal on the other (*rev.*), both by J. Croker. An interesting medal dated 1708 and 1716, with a portrait of Prince James, the 'Old Pretender' (*obv.*), and a map (*rev.*), recalls the unsuccessful invasion attempts in those years, with the inscription (trans.) 'accomplishing nothing' / 'twice he came, he saw, he did not conquer, and he returned in tears' (**216**). In 1717 the Act of Grace was passed, granting an amnesty and free pardon to those who had taken part in rebellions. J. Croker designed a medal with a bust of George I (*obv.*), and Clemency touching a serpent's head with a caduceus (*rev.*).

Continuing attacks by Spanish colonists on British shipping in Central America during the 1730s culminated in victories at Portobello in 1739 and at Carthagena in 1741, both widely acclaimed in England, along with the expeditions' commander Admiral Edward Vernon. A large number of medals were made, a few in silver, bronze and lead, but more than eighty different types in pinchbeck (**65, 217**). Many have differing die combinations and are varieties from a small pool of general designs, which typically portray Vernon, sometimes accompanied by his second-in-command, Commodore Brown, and the inscriptions 'Admiral Vernon and Commodore Brown' (*obv.*), 'Took Portobello with six ships only Nov. 22 1739', with a group of ships entering harbour (*rev.*).

Jacobite attempts at securing the throne in the 1740s are recalled by many medals. The capture of their garrison at Carlisle in 1745 by the Duke of Cumberland is commemorated by a cheaply-produced medal: with a bust of the Duke (*obv.*), and the Duke holding a shield with the King's portrait, attacking a hydra (*rev.*). The last big battle at which the Jacobites fought was Culloden in 1746, where the Duke again commanded on behalf of his father, George II, and for which at least fifteen medals were struck. One has an equestrian figure of the Duke brandishing a sword (*obv.*), and is coupled with two reverses: on one, Prince Charles the 'Young Pretender', tries to seize a crown on a column, but is pulled back by the Duke and run through with a sword, with the inscription 'come back again pretender'; the other has an execution scene and the inscription 'more rebels a comeing'. The collapse of the Jacobite uprising is also shown on a medal with a bust of the Duke (*obv.*), and a Highlander kneeling before the rampant lion of England (*rev.*) (**218**). An interesting medal dated 1749, with a Highlander facing, sword drawn, (*obv.*), and an expanded rose (*rev.*), shows undiminished Jacobite resolve, with the inscriptions (trans.) 'who can contend with me' / 'my affairs are at issue' (**219**).

The Royal Society of Arts sponsored medals commemorating British victories in the 1750s and 1760s, including those at Louisburg in 1758, Minden in 1759 and Montreal in 1760 (**220**); that at Louisburg was celebrated by several medals (**221**). The various naval actions at Gibraltar during the eighteenth century are commemorated by many medals. Its capture in 1704 is shown on a medal with Queen Anne (*obv.*), and Neptune offering his trident to Britannia (*rev.*), by J. Croker. Its siege in 1782, and relief in 1783, is celebrated by several portrait medals, including those depicting its defender General Eliott. One, by L. Pingo, pays tribute to the 'zealous exertion of patience perseverance and intrepidity . . . [and the garrison who in 1783] . . . triumphed over the combined powers of France and Spain' (*obv.*), with a detailed plan of the bay of Gibraltar, delineating the positions of batteries and ships (*rev.*) (**222**).

Admiral Rodney's victories against the French in the West Indies in 1781 made him a popular hero. Several medals commemorate his actions at St Eustatius and the capture of ships from the Dutch, and carry the slogan 'Rodney for Ever', which was also used on commemorative ceramics. Uniform medals by J.G. Hancock commemorate British naval actions at Helvoetsluys in 1796, Cape St Vincent in 1797, Camperdown in 1797, Tory Island and the Nile, both in 1798, and Trafalgar in 1805: with the respective commanding officer and a complementary reverse. The three prominent naval actions from this period, 'The Glorious First of June' in 1794, under Admiral the Earl Howe, and Nelson's victories at the Nile in 1798 and Trafalgar in 1805 (**223**), are together commemorated by more than forty medals. Alexander Davison, a confidant of Nelson, presented medals as personal rewards to seamen and officers of the various ranks who had fought at the Nile: a figure of Hope holds an oval medallion of Nelson (*obv.*), with a view of the British fleet assembled in Aboukir Bay, with the inscription 'Almighty God has blessed his Majesty's arms' (*rev.*) (**224**), by C.H. Küchler. A medal commemorating Trafalgar, also by Küchler, with a uniformed bust of Nelson (*obv.*), and a panoramic view of the naval engagement and the inscription 'England expects every man will do his duty' (*rev.*) (**75**), was struck and presented by Matthew Boulton to those who had taken part. Both the Davison and Boulton medals sometimes occur with the recipient and ship's name unofficially inscribed.

A series of forty medals published by James Mudie (*An Historical and Critical Account of a Grand Series of National Medals,* London, 1820) commemorate British victories since 1794. The Duke of Wellington is well represented, as are his officers and their actions. One by T. Webb/ N. Brenet commemorates Lord Beresford's command at Albuera in 1811, with his uniformed bust (*obv.*), and a Polish lancer attacking a British infantryman (*rev.*). Lord Hill's triumph at Almarez in 1812, is celebrated: with his bust (*obv.*), and Victory and Bellona flying over a destroyed bridge (*rev.*), by G. Mills/R. Gayrard. A medal by T. Webb/ G. Mills celebrates Lieutenant-General Picton's victory at Badajoz in 1812, with his uniformed bust (*obv.*), and the British standard (*rev.*). One of the last medals of Mudie's series commemorates the capture of Algiers in 1816 (225), by L. Brenet/Gérard. The Battle of Waterloo in 1815 is commemorated by more than twenty medals, a few of which carry portraits of both Wellington and his ally Field-Marshal Blücher.

Actions in the Crimean War 1854–6, most notably at Alma, Balaklava and Inkermann, are commemorated on uniform medals, struck by Pinches, with a view of the respective engagement (*obv.*), and details of the regiments (*rev.*). An interesting medal by Allen and Moore depicts Admiral Napier standing on the deck of the *Duke of Wellington*, with the inscription 'Lads, war is declared', the beginning of Napier's much-criticized response to the declaration of war with Russia (which continued 'with a numerous and bold enemy. Should they meet us and offer battle, you know how to dispose of them') (*obv.*), with a broadside view of the ship (*rev.*) (226). Florence Nightingale and Lord Raglan, commander of the British forces in the Crimea, are both commemorated on portrait medals of 1855 by Pinches. They also struck a medal commemorating the Indian Mutiny in 1857, with the standing figure of Justice, and a dedication to 'the brave defenders of our Indian Empire' (*obv.*). More than 23,000 people had attended a fast day held at Crystal Palace on 7 October 1857, in memory of the mutiny and massacre of 211 women and children at Cawnpore.

The emotions which the South African (Boer) War aroused are evident from the number of medals struck in Britain, as well as those on the Continent, many of which are of anti-British sentiment. Portrait medals commemorate the various commanders and their campaigns, such as Lord Roberts at Bloemfontein and Pretoria and Lord Baden-Powell at Mafeking (227), both in 1900. Others include General White (228), General Redvers Buller and Lord Kitchener. A medal of 1901 by F. Bowcher symbolizes, both in its size (100 mm) and imagery, the apotheosis of the British Empire: with a bust of Edward VII (*obv.*), and an equestrian portrait of Roberts, lauded by Fame and Victory (*rev.*). Specific actions fought by the City of London Imperial Volunteers are listed on a medal, with Londinia welcoming a soldier (*obv.*), and both the Union and C.I.V. flags upon a hill (*rev.*), by G. Frampton. The Boer War was the first conflict for which towns and districts in Britain, Canada and Australia, some with small and closely-knit communities, presented medals in tribute to their local boys who had gone out to fight; they were often inscribed with a name and awarded at a special ceremony on the homecoming.

Few medals commemorating the First World War were struck in Britain, in comparison to those produced on the Continent, particularly in France and Germany. Apart from the medals arising out of the Royal Numismatic Society's competition to celebrate the naval victory at Jutland Bank, three other medals also commemorate the victory as well as those at Heligoland Bight and Dogger Bank, all between 1914–16. They were designed by Prince Louis of Battenberg, Marquess of Milford Haven

PLATE 29

PLATE 30

(himself a collector of naval medals), and sold by Spink's in aid of Naval Orphanages. Medals of Lord Kitchener were produced by French and Swiss medallists: one carries Kitchener's uniformed bust (*obv.*) (**229**), with Britannia portrayed as Minerva calling her sons to arms, as did Kitchener (whose image on the famous poster was captioned 'Your Country Needs You') (*rev.*), by J.P. Legastelois. A Belgian portrait medal by A. Bonnetain commemorates Dr Marie Depage and the English nurse Edith Cavell, who was shot by the Germans for espionage in 1915. A small group of medals record German prisoner-of-war camps at Douglas and Knockaloe (Isle of Man), Islington (London), Stobs (Scotland) and Wakefield (Yorkshire) (**230**). They all have German inscriptions and are similar in style, but it is unclear where and by whom they were made. The Armistice in 1918 and Peace in 1919 saw the issue of large numbers of medals by districts and townships throughout Britain and the Commonwealth. Like the tribute medals of the Boer War, many were given to soldiers on their return.

Even fewer medals, tribute or otherwise, commemorate the Second World War. One marks the various battles over London, with aircraft over the Tower (*obv.*), and St Paul's Cathedral (*rev.*), by Pinches, and sold in aid of the Royal Air Force Benevolent Fund. The actions of the First Airborne Division at Arnhem in 1944 are recalled on a medal by L.O. Wenckebach, showing a fallen warrior (*obv.*), and an armed and helmeted warrior (*rev.*), and sold in aid of the Airborne Forces' Charity Society. Another medal dated 1944–5 commemorates the xxx Corps' 'crossing of the Rhine' (*obv.*), and the 'final advance into Germany' (*rev.*).

Art and science

The Arts are well represented with portrait medals, although the imagery suggested by subjects such as music and literature may not, itself, be readily conveyed. One of the earliest of the thirty or more portrait medals of William Shakespeare dates to *c.* 1740, with his bust (*obv.*), and a landscape scene, the inscription 'wild above rule and art' (*rev.*), by J. Dassier. A jubilee in 1769 is recalled on a medal which may have served as a pass for the celebrations at Stratford: with Shakespeare's portrait (*obv.*), the inscription includes the first medallic reference to the actor-manager David Garrick (*rev.*). In 1911, William Sharp Ogden wished to record an unusual Shakespeare portrait on a painting that he had obtained, and commissioned a medal by F. Bowcher with this portrait (*obv.*), and the muse of Poesy casually laureating Shakespeare's head (*rev.*) (**231**). The majority of Shakespeare medals, however, commemorate the anniversaries of his birth, celebrated in 1864 and 1964.

Lord Byron left England in 1816, and subsequently joined Greek insurgents in their struggle for independence from Turkish rule. His colourful life cast a romantic shadow and turned him into a cult figure. Several portrait medals were made after his death in 1824 at the age of thirty-six. The inscription on a fine medal, issued as a tribute from a London publisher, is in Greek. Byron's bare head is depicted (*obv.*) (**232**), with a bay-tree, unscathed from a bolt of lightning, the immortality of which is likened to his fame (*rev.*), by A. J. Stothard. Sir Walter Scott, the Scottish poet and historical novelist, is commemorated by several portrait medals. One struck at the time of his death in 1832 has an embodiment of the *Lady of the Lake* (*rev.*), by W. Bain. A portrait medal of William Wordsworth (**233**), designed by L.C. Wyon and struck in 1848, is inscribed 'friend of the wise and teacher of the good' (*rev.*).

A non-portrait prize medal by R. Yeo, dated 1750, commemorates both the Academy of Ancient Music and John Christopher Pepusch, a founder-member and German composer who, like George Frederick Handel, had come over to England in the eighteenth century. A medal of Handel himself (*obv.*) (**234**), with an inscription in a wreath (*rev.*), was struck in 1784 on the centenary of his birth, for which concerts were held in London. Edward Elgar is commemorated on a medal *c.* 1905 by P.W. Hedley. The seventieth birthday of Hans Richter, a Hungarian conductor who worked in England, at times with Elgar, is commemorated on a medal by H.W. Page struck in 1913.

Medals commemorating painters include those of Sir Joshua Reynolds (**235**) and the miniaturist John Smart, both by J. Kirk and struck in the 1770s. One of Benjamin West is a tribute in 1820 from the medallist G. Mills, 'in grateful remembrance of the paternal solicitude . . . of his first patron Benjamin West' (*rev.*). The Art Union of London series includes portraits of William Hogarth of 1848, by L.C. Wyon; Thomas Gainsborough of 1859, by E. Ortner; and J.M.W. Turner of 1876, by L.C. Wyon. Each carries an illustration of their work (*rev.*).

Actors to have been commemorated include Thomas Ryder in 1786 by W. Mossop, and the celebrated actor-managers David Garrick in 1772 by L. Pingo, and John Philip Kemble in 1798 by J.G. Hancock (**236**). A portrait medal of the comedian Joseph Munden, also by Hancock, was struck on his fortieth birthday in 1799, and carries the epithet 'exposer of folly and dispellor of spleen . . . to cheer the sinking heart and create a moral life is all that philosophy can teach the mind' (*rev.*). In 1844, Tom Thumb (Charles Stratton), the celebrated dwarf, was exhibited in London by the showman Phinaeus T. Barnum, whose name as publisher appears on several medals. They usually feature Tom Thumb standing on a desk amongst books and an inkwell (*obv.*), to which is coupled either the conjoined busts of his parents, or the equipment in which he was transported (*rev.*), by Allen and Moore. A portrait medal, by J. Moore, of the magician John Henry Anderson, refers to the 'Great Wizard of the North', and informs us that he was 'commanded to perform before her majesty Queen Victoria at Balmoral Castle August 28, 1849'.

A cast uniface medal of Lillie Langtry by E. J. Poynter, *c.* 1882, has her bust almost facing, a miniature dagger in her cleavage, a pointed reference to the dramatic. Several medals were struck in 1905 on the death of Henry Irving. On one, by F. Bowcher, he is portrayed in his last role as Tennyson's *Becket* (*obv.*), with the epitaph 'mighty magician, master of the spells that move to grief or pity, love or scorn' (*rev.*) (**237**). Sybil Thorndike's role in 1923 of Shaw's *Saint Joan* is portrayed on a uniface cast medal by M. Kitchener. A very fine cast medal of Laurence Olivier was made by F. Kormis in 1949 (*see* **fig. 23**).

Medals recording developments in the fields of science and the humanities include a broad range of subjects. Within that of civil engineering, for example, there are a large number of medals which illustrate bridges, railways and similar technical achievements. That which commemorates the opening in 1808 of Dunkeld bridge in Scotland is one of the earliest such medals with, typically, a view of its span (*obv.*), and details of dimensions and cost (*rev.*). Important bridges commemorated include the Newcastle-on-Tyne high level bridge in 1849 (**238**), and the Clifton suspension bridge in 1864 (**239**). That for the Forth bridge in 1890 has a perspective view of the cantilever bridge (*obv.*), and its dimensions (*rev.*), by L.C. Lauer. The medal for Tower Bridge in 1894 has the conjoined busts of Queen Victoria and the Prince and Princess of Wales (*obv.*), with a view of the bridge (*rev.*), by F. Bowcher; this is a Corporation of London medal, and a demonstrative statement of Victorian engineering.

Among early railway medals are those for the Liverpool – Manchester railway in 1830. Several illustrate the bridge at Newton, with a locomotive crossing (*obv.*), and a view of the railway emerging from the tunnel at Liverpool Station (*rev.*). Many are by T. Halliday and were published in Liverpool, where they were sold as souvenirs. The Gloucester and Cheltenham Railway is commemorated on a medal *c.* 1830, with a locomotive pulling passengers and freight in three open wagons, a barge on a canal in the foreground (*obv.*), with the inscription recording the *Royal William* locomotive (*rev.*) (**275**). Several medals commemorate the opening in 1837 of the Birmingham–Liverpool–Manchester Grand Junction railway (**240**), some of which tabulate distances, journey times, and their respective destinations. Euston Arch, sadly demolished in recent years, is the main feature on a medal for the London–Birmingham railway in 1838, on which occurs the earliest medallic reference to Robert Stephenson, its engineer. The opening in 1840 of the Newcastle–Carlisle Railway is commemorated on a fine medal by W. Wyon: with a view of a town and landscape, between which there is a train crossing a viaduct (*obv.*), and the two city shields (*rev.*). Medals were also struck to commemorate the opening of branch lines, such as those at South Devon in 1855, Solway Junction, Annan in 1865 and North Cornwall in 1893. The centenary in 1925 of the Stockton–Darlington railway is commemorated on a rugged medal by G. Bayes, with the conjoined busts of George

Stephenson and Edward Pearse, the railway projector who adopted Stephenson's plans (*obv.*), and a locomotive from both periods (*rev.*).

Developments in marine engineering, such as the building of canals, inland channels and docks, are well documented. Brighton Pier is illustrated on the reverse of a medal by B. Wyon, which recalls Samuel Brown, its engineer and 'commander in his majesty's navy', who developed special links for the chain cables used in its construction. An interesting medal of John Rennie, the civil engineer (*obv.*), provides both overhead and cross-sectional views of Sheerness docks and basin, opened in 1823 (*rev.*) (**241**), by W. Bain. The opening of a navigable channel to Newport, and the deepening of the river Tees between Stockton and the sea, in 1831, are commemorated on Ottley's medal, with illustrations of shipping (**276**). The Brunels, father and son, are among the most prominent nineteenth-century civil engineers. Marc Isambard Brunel is recorded on the large number of medals commemorating the completion and opening of the Thames Tunnel in 1842–3, with which he is most commonly associated (**277**). Isambard Kingdom Brunel, his son, was responsible for other engineering projects, including the building of the steamships *Great Britain* in 1843 (**278**), and *Great Eastern* in 1858.

Joseph Priestley, the scientist, philosopher and 'discoverer' of oxygen, carried out a number of experiments in gases, as recalled on a medal by J.G. Hancock dated 1783, with his portrait (*obv.*), and apparatus (*rev.*) (**242**). Charles Hutton computed the mean density of the Earth, and is commemorated on a medal of 1821 by B. Wyon: with his portrait (*obv.*), and a globe and ball suspended from a rule, and a cannon suspended from a quadrant (*rev.*). Edward Thomason's series of sixteen scientific medals, some with illustrations, trace developments in fields such as metallurgy, mineralogy, optics and phrenology (**243**). A medal struck in 1883 commemorates Joseph Whitworth (*obv.*), and his invention of a machine capable of measuring the distance of one millionth of an inch (*rev.*), by E.J. Poynter. Other portrait medals of scientists include those of Robert Boyle, Humphrey Davy, Michael Faraday, Edmund Halley (**244**) and Isaac Newton. The romance of early balloon flight is recorded by several medals such as that dated 1784, depicting Vincent Lundardi, an Italian working in England, who is referred to as the 'first aerial traveller in England' (*obv.*), and a balloon above clouds (*rev.*) (**273**). A portrait medal of James Sadler tells, in 1811, of the 'first English aeronaut' (*obv.*), with a balloon and two men in its gondola (*rev.*) (**274**), by P. Wyon.

Medical practitioners and developments in medical science are extensively commemorated. A cast medal of 1724 recalls Starkey Myddelton, a man-midwife. It shows a naked boy and girl standing upon a pedestal (*obv.*), and the armorial shield of Myddelton (*rev.*), whose published papers in the Royal Society's *Philosophical Transactions* include an account 'of a child being taken out of the abdomen after having lain there for upwards

PLATE 31

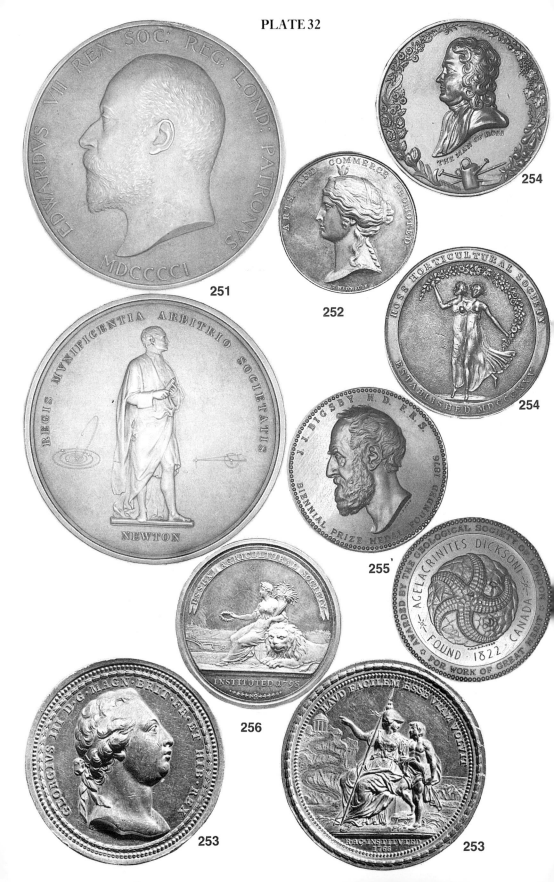

PLATE 32

251

252

254

254

255

256

253

253

of sixteen years, during which time the woman had four children, all born alive'. An interesting medal from the mid eighteenth century both advertises and illustrates the services of Thomas Birch, surgeon and man-midwife: with a leg amputation scene (*obv.*), and a reference to midwifery (*rev.*) (**245**). A portrait medal dated 1779 of the surgeon Peter Clare (*obv.*), recalls his treatment of venereal disease by the absorption of medicine through the mouth (*rev.*) (**246**), by T. Holloway. Edward Jenner's development of the vaccine is commemorated on a portrait medal of 1796 by F. Loos, with Hygeia protecting an infant from a demon (*rev.*) (**247**). James Morison, self-styled medical reformer and vendor of universal medicines, is commemorated on a portrait medal by T.R. Pinches dated 1840 (*obv.*), recalling the principles 'that all diseases arise from impurity of the blood . . . that such impurity can only be eradicated by a purgative such as the vegetable universal medicine . . . that the deadly poisons used as medicines by the doctors are totally unnecessary in the cure of diseases' (*rev.*).

Architects and their work appear on many medals. A fine cast portrait medal of Christopher Wren (*obv.*), has a view of the west front of St Paul's Cathedral (*rev.*), by G.D. Gaab; a fitting tribute and the only contemporary medal, made at or soon after his death in 1723. The Art Union of London series includes portraits of architects with examples of their work on the reverse, including Inigo Jones' Banqueting Hall, by C.F. Carter in 1849; William Chambers' Somerset House, by B. Wyon in 1857 (**88**); and Charles Barry's Houses of Parliament, by J. and L. Wiener in 1862. The Corporation of London series contains several superbly detailed interior views, including the Coal Exchange in 1849 by B. Wyon (**82**), St Paul's Cathedral in 1872 by J.S. and A.B. Wyon (**248**), and the Guildhall in 1886 by Elkington (**249**). A large series of architectural medals by the Wiener brothers illustrates interior and exterior views of several English churches and cathedrals, such as those at Lincoln, Winchester and York, as well as others throughout Europe.

Joseph Paxton is commemorated on various medals illustrating his celebrated Crystal Palace, opened in 1851 for the Great Exhibition, several of which enumerate its dimensions. In 1854, it was dismantled and re-erected on a permanent site at Sydenham, south-east London, where its enlargement was supervised by Paxton, and commemorated once again with medals (**90**). Francis Fowke planned the International Exhibition building in 1862 and drew up the original plans for the Royal Albert Hall in 1871. He is commemorated on a superb high-relief portrait medal by G.T. Morgan (**250**), established by the Royal Engineers as an architectural prize on his death in 1865. Thomas Leverton Donaldson had close links with both architecture and numismatics; a founder member of the Royal Institute of British Architects, he designed their device, which happens to appear on their 1834 Honorary Medal by B. Wyon. A portrait medal of Donaldson, by J.S. and A.B. Wyon, was struck on his retirement as Professor of Architecture at University College London in 1865 and used as an award. Donaldson was the author of *Architectura Numismatica*, 1859, which discusses buildings depicted on classical coins, and served on the committee of the Art Union of London.

Several medals commemorate the related disciplines of antiquities, archaeology and numismatics. William Stukeley, a physician and rector famous for his study of Stonehenge, wrote extensively on antiquities and numismatics, and is commemorated by an interesting cast medal dated 1765, with his portrait (*obv.*), and an illustration of Stonehenge (*rev.*). John Evans, the archaeologist and numismatist, published numerous papers on both subjects. He was president of the Royal Numismatic Society from 1874 until his death in 1908, and appears on a medal by Pinches marking the Society's golden jubilee in 1887. Charles Roach Smith, the antiquary and archaeologist, is commemorated on a portrait medal (*obv.*) presented, just three days before he died, by the Society of Antiquaries 'from fellow antiquaries and friends in recognition of lifelong services to archaeology 1890' (*rev.*), by Pinches. Roach Smith was also a frequent contributor to the *Numismatic Chronicle*, and in 1883 became the first recipient of the Royal Numismatic Society's medal.

Developments in arts and sciences, manufactures and commerce, were to be seen at many exhibitions. Those for which medals have been struck include the Great Exhibition in 1851, the Fine Arts and Treasures Exhibition in Manchester in 1857, the Colonial and Indian Exhibition in London in 1886, the British Empire Exhibition of 1924–5 at Wembley and the Festival of Britain in 1951. Smaller exhibitions were held throughout Britain, variously entitled Apprentices, Arts and Crafts, Fine Art, Local Manufactures, Industrial, and many of these have also been commemorated by medals.

The presentation medal

Medals have been used in many spheres as a means to both reward and encourage. When presented, they normally have an inscription engraved on the edge or in a space provided by the design. The number of societies, institutions, government agencies, and local authorities, which have awarded medals over the last 250 years can be counted in the hundreds.

One of the first to award medals was the Royal Society (of London). In 1736, funds from a bequest made by Sir Godfrey Copley M.P. were used to create a gold medal, presented annually for the most significant contribution to the advancement of natural science. The Copley Medal (**56**), by J.S. Tanner, is the Royal Society's highest award, and was presented continuously until the 1950s, when replaced by a new design, awarded in gilt silver. The Society instituted other awards, the most prominent of which is the Royal Medal, established largely through the endeavours of Sir Robert Peel. Since 1833, two Royal medals have been awarded annually in gold for important contributions to the advancement of natural knowledge, each in a triennial cycle of subjects. It has the reigning sovereign's portrait (*obv.*), with Sir Isaac Newton's statue at Trinity College, Cambridge (*rev.*) (**251**), the first three issues, of George IV, William IV and Victoria, by W. Wyon. Until 1939, recipients also received a replica in silver, which was usually 'frosted', set within two watch-style glasses, and bound by a silver frame. The Royal Society has also awarded portrait medals in memory of eminent scientists, such as the (Charles) Darwin Medal, by A. Wyon; awarded in silver biennially from 1890 for biological research.

The Royal Society of Arts, instituted in 1754, has awarded a number of different medals in gold and silver, and latterly bronze, for aspects of design and application in arts, manufactures and commerce: the Mercury and Minerva Medal (from 1758, for all three categories) by T. Pingo; the Isis Medal (from 1810, for fine arts) by T. Wyon Jr. (**252**); the Ceres Medal (from 1813, for agriculture) by W. Wyon; and the Vulcan Medal (from 1818, for mechanics) by G. Mills. These medals were replaced by the Patron or President's Medal, by W. Wyon/L.C. Wyon, awarded since *c.* 1853 in gold and silver, and latterly also in bronze. The Albert Medal, by L.C. Wyon, is the Society's highest award, and has been presented annually in gold since 1864 for outstanding contributions in arts, manufactures and commerce.

The Royal Dublin Society was founded in 1731 for the improvement of husbandry, manufactures and other applications of arts and sciences. Since the 1760s, it has awarded more than twenty-five prize medals, most frequently during the nineteenth century. Two commonly used obverse designs were the Society's arms and the seated figure of Minerva, each coupled with a wreath (*rev.*). The Society's (Robert) Boyle Medal, with a bust of Boyle (*obv.*), and a seated figure of Minerva (*rev.*), by A.G. Wyon, was presented from 1899 in bronze for scientific contributions.

The Royal Academy of Arts, instituted in 1768, awarded two different medals, both by T. Pingo. Each has the reigning sovereign's portrait (**253**), coupled with two different reverses: that with a torso (based on the Belvedere torso in the Vatican) was awarded annually from 1768 in silver, and later also in bronze, by the Royal Academy Schools for students; the other, with Minerva seated (**253**), was awarded annually in gold, in the disciplines of architecture, painting, and sculpture, until 1772, and biennially thereafter. In 1830, the reverse of this medal was replaced by an allegory of the three disciplines for which the medal, now by W. Wyon, was given. In the 1930s a new design, with a bust of George III wearing a tricorn (*obv.*), and a laurel branch (*rev.*), by E. Gillick, replaced all other medals.

The Horticultural Society of London was founded in 1804 and designated 'Royal' in 1861. Their Foundation Medal by G.F. Pidgeon was awarded from 1811, in gold, silver and bronze: a large greenhouse (*obv.*), and the god of gardens decked with flowers by Flora and offered fruits by Pomona (*rev.*). The Society's Banksian Medal, by W. Wyon, was presented from 1820 in silver and bronze: with a bust of Joseph Banks (*obv.*), and an inscription (*rev.*). Several recently-established horticultural societies were also presenting medals, including those at Aylesbury in 1821, Cambridge in 1824, Berkshire in 1831, Guernsey in 1832 and Henley in 1833. An interesting medal awarded by the Ross Horticultural Society, *c.* 1825, has a portrait of John Kyrle, the landscape and town planner who developed Ross-on-Wye, on which he is referred to as 'The Man of Ross' (*obv.*), with two female figures (*rev.*) (**254**). Several botanic societies established at this time also awarded medals, including those at Birmingham, Durham, Jersey and Liverpool. The reverses of their medals were often coupled with an obverse portrait of Carl Linné (Linnaeus), whose system of plant classification was itself the subject of a medal (**78**).

The growth of the agricultural industry in the latter part of the eighteenth century can be measured to some extent by the many societies which began to award medals, such as the Notts. and W. Riding of Yorks in 1765, Salford Hundred in 1767, Glamorgan in 1772, Richmond in 1778 and Essex in 1793 (**256**). From *c.* 1800, the Board of Agriculture presented medals for various improvements in the social conditions of the labouring classes, such as a leather substitute for shoes, and inventions in husbandry. These medals were by C.H. Küchler and carried a bust of George III (*obv.*), and a female figure holding a spade entwined with a serpent (*rev.*) (**257**). A large number of local agricultural societies awarded medals throughout Britain during the nineteenth century, including those at Ayrshire, Cork, Devon (**258**), Dumfries, Farnham, Liverpool, Merioneth, Navan, Newry, Renfrewshire, Staffordshire, Waterford, Wexford and Yorkshire.

The Royal Academy of Music, instituted in 1822, awarded silver and bronze medals during the nineteenth century and later: with a bust of Apollo (*obv.*), and a wreath (*rev.*), by B. Wyon. In 1859 the Sacred Harmonic Society organized a Handel Centenary Festival at Crystal Palace, attended by more than 25,000 people. Stewards and performers were awarded bronze medals designed by W.J. Taylor, with a portrait of Handel (*obv.*), and an inscription in wreath (*rev.*). At their fiftieth and last season in 1882, the Society presented silver and bronze medals by Pinches, depicting an open music score of 'The Messiah' (*obv.*), and a statue of Handel (*rev.*).

The Institution of Civil Engineers was given a bequest by Thomas Telford, the civil engineer, for the award of various annual premiums. The first medal, by W. Wyon, was awarded from 1837 in gold, silver and bronze and carried a bust of Telford (*obv.*), and a view of his Menai Strait suspension bridge (*rev.*). Other prizes presented by the Institution include the (James) Watt and (George) Stephenson medals.

The Geological Society of London presented several prize medals, the first of which commemorates the physicist and chemist, William Hyde Wollaston, who endowed a medal by W. Wyon. This was awarded annually from 1831 for research into the mineral structure of the earth, and was presented in gold, and palladium, which Wollaston had discovered. The (John) Bigsby Medal of 1876, with his portrait (*obv.*), and a starfish (*rev.*) (**255**), by J.S. and A.B. Wyon, was awarded biennially in gold, and latterly bronze, for geological work. From 1847, the Zoological Society of London presented an attractive medal featuring twelve species of birds (*obv.*), and seven of animals (*rev.*), by B. Wyon. The first silver medal was for the introduction of European bison; medals in gold were given for special services, while bronze went to keepers.

At the Great Exhibition in 1851, five different medals – the Council (*see* Frontispiece), Prize, Juror's, Services and Exhibitor's (in descending order of size and status) – were awarded, some in a number of classes. The first three carry conjoined portraits of Victoria and Albert by W. Wyon (*obv.*), and allegories of Industry, Commerce and Britannia, by J.F. Domard, L.C. Wyon (*see* **fig. 16**) and G.G. Adams respectively (*rev.*). The Services and Exhibitor's medals (**87**), also by W. Wyon, each have a bust of Prince Albert (*obv.*), with an inscription in wreath, and a globe in wreath, respectively (*rev.*). The Great Exhibition paved the way for others at which medals were awarded, such as the International Exhibition in London in 1862 (**259**), as well as those at Maidenhead and Plymouth in 1865, Lichfield in 1874, Exeter in 1882, Glasgow in 1886, Sheffield in 1892 and Belfast in 1895.

The medal has also played an important role in education; as a tool of encouragement and merit, it provided an example for others to emulate. Wholly engraved medals, usually of circular or oval form, were given in silver to pupils at private schools and academies *c.* 1750–1850. They are amongst the earliest of school medals, and occupy a small but interesting place in the genre. Struck medals have been awarded by schools, colleges, and learning establishments of every kind since the eighteenth century, their numbers reaching a peak in the nineteenth century. The Department of Education was set up in the 1850s to assimilate a structure of formal education throughout the country, and awarded medals as a form of encouragement.

Christ's Hospital school presented a medal from *c.* 1790, given in silver to a 'marker', whose function was to supervise the behaviour of boys: with a bust of Edward VI, its founder (*obv.*), and an open Bible (*rev.*), by L. Pingo. Winchester College has an equally long tradition for presenting medals, beginning with two, usually awarded in silver and both with the bust of William of Wykeham, the school's founder (*obv.*): the first, from *c.* 1770, has a wreath (*rev.*), by R. Yeo; that awarded from 1797 has the Prince of Wales' plumes (*rev.*), by J. Milton. From the reign of William IV a series of royal medals were awarded, usually in silver, and carrying the bust of the sovereign (*obv.*), and William of Wykeham's tomb (*rev.*) (**102**).

In the 1790s, the Historical Society of Dublin awarded silver medals for history, oratory and poetry; they were of a standard design by W. Mossop and showed female figures symbolizing those disciplines (*obv.*), coupled with one of three reverses, according to the discipline. Trinity College Dublin first awarded medals during the eighteenth century. Those most commonly presented were given during the mid nineteenth century, for a variety of subjects, each with a standard bust of Elizabeth I, who conferred a grant for the erection of the college (*obv.*), with its shield (*rev.*). These medals, originally by W. Woodhouse, were made in different sizes and awarded in gold, silver and bronze (**260**).

The Department of Science and Art, an amalgamation of the Departments of both Practical Art, and Science and Art, was established in 1856, as originally proposed by the Royal Commissioners of the Great Exhibition. It presented medals at public examinations in eight main groups of subjects, the intention being to encourage and stimulate talent amongst the industrial classes at schools throughout Britain. Their medals carry a diademed bust of Queen Victoria (*obv.*), and an inscription within a wreath (*rev.*), by W. Wyon. They were presented in gold, silver and bronze, and in different sizes. Similar medals were also awarded by the National Art Training School (**261**) and the Board of Education.

In 1878, the City and Guilds of London Institute, established by City of London Companies, awarded medals from *c.* 1880 in silver and bronze, for the advancement of technical education. Its first issue carries the City of London shield (*obv.*), and a panel within an inscription (*rev.*), by E.D. Jackman. The Prince of Wales became its President and a medal was introduced *c.* 1890, with his bust (*obv.*), and a panel within an inscription (*rev.*), by L.C. Wyon. A similar medal was struck in 1901 on his accession as Edward VII, when he became the Institute's Patron. The panel on the reverses of these medals would contain details of the grade.

Between *c.* 1888 and 1925, local education authorities throughout Britain awarded medals annually for punctuality and good attendance, most usually in white metal and bronze. A large number, by F. Ransom, were awarded by the London County Council (**262**), which commonly have a suspension bar to which are attached clasps bearing the years of its award.

One of the most striking medals for medicine is that of William Cheselden, with his bust in surgeon's cap (*obv.*), and a cadaver on a table awaiting dissection, its muscles and sinews clearly visible (*rev.*), by W. Wyon. It was awarded in silver by St Thomas' Hospital for surgical anatomy, 1829–*c.* 1845, and is among several which they presented,

PLATE 33

259

257

258

261

260

262

263

264

263

PLATE 34

272

268

265

269

266

271

267

270

Many other hospitals have awarded medals, including St Bartholomew's Hospital, whose (Alfred) Willett Medal by F. Bowcher was awarded for surgery. This carries his bust (*obv.*), and the hospital's façade (*rev.*) (**263**). From *c.* 1870, Glasgow University's medical faculty awarded portrait medals of Joseph Black, William Cullen, William Gairdner, John Hunter (**264**) and William Hunter (*obv.*), each with a uniform inscription (*rev.*), by N. Macphail; they were awarded in silver and bronze, for anatomy, pathology, physiology and surgery.

Governor-generals of Canada presented medals during the nineteenth century and later, usually in silver, and sometimes in gold; to supervisory staff and members of the household, for loyal service or on retirement from office. They comprise conjoined portraits of the couple (they all appear to have been married) (*obv.*), and a personal coat of arms (*rev.*). The first medal, by J.S. and A.B. Wyon, was presented by the Earl of Dufferin, whose installation took place in 1872. Viceroys of India awarded medals, consisting of three main types: the first issue is similar to the governor-general medal; the second carries a coat of arms (*obv.*), and an open wreath (*rev.*); the third, a coat of arms (*obv.*), palm trees and the breast star of the Order of the Star of India (*rev.*). A variation of that presented in 1884 by the first viceroy has a coronet surmounting the collar of the Order of St Patrick (*obv.*), and a coat of arms (*rev.*).

A large variety of medals has been awarded in connection with sport. That of curling has a relatively long tradition, dating to the eighteenth century. Not surprisingly, many are Scottish and occur both struck and entirely engraved, some with a scene of a game in progress, the edge mounted with miniature brooms and curling stones. Archery is another sport for which medals were awarded throughout the nineteenth century, again, in both struck and engraved form. A commonly-found example of the former has a bust of the goddess Diana (*obv.*), and a target (*rev.*), an attached ribbon displaying clasps carrying the date and place of competition. A large number of university prize medals, particularly those of Oxford and Cambridge, were awarded for activities such as athletics, chess, cycling (**265**) and rowing during the 1870–1920 period. Medals usually carry a shield (*obv.*), and a device or inscription (*rev.*). They commonly occur within two watch-style glasses, bound with a silver frame; or in a fitted case, on the inside lid of which is sewn a silver or bronze plaque inscribed with details.

The most glamorous of all sports' prize medals are those of the Olympic Games. Since the first meeting in Athens in 1896, both commemorative and prize medals have been struck for each of the games, including those held in London in 1908 and 1948. The 1908 prize medals were awarded for various classes, in gold, silver and bronze. On these, a youth stands facing, crowned with a wreath held by two female figures (*obv.*), while Fame leads a warrior, as St George slays the dragon (*rev.*) (**97**), by

B. Mackennal. The 1948 medal, by G. Cassioli, was again given in three metals: Victory holds a wreath aloft (*obv.*), with a competitor chaired in victory by athletes (*rev.*). This design had been used since the Amsterdam games in 1928, with the inscription on the die being altered according to the host city.

The growth of interest in social and fashionable activities during the late nineteenth century is evident from the numbers of medals being awarded, such as those by numerous photographic clubs and societies throughout Britain. These medals date between *c*. 1890–1930 and were presented, usually in bronze or silver, for photographic exhibits and lantern slides and frequently include a camera in the design. Other popular pastimes for which medals were awarded include pigeon-fancying and dog-breeding. The introduction to Britain of exotic breeds of domestic cats only started to take place at the end of the century (**292**), a time when the National Cat Club began to hold exhibitions and award medals (**293**).

The Royal Humane Society, founded in 1774, awarded medals to those who, at personal risk, saved or attempted to save life. The standard design shows a naked boy attempting to breathe life into a torch (*obv.*), and a wreath (*rev.*). A number of dies were used in the striking of these medals, the first of which is by L. Pingo, awarded in silver between *c*. 1775–1820, and subsequently in both silver and bronze. The Society also instituted a silver medal, given from 1882 for proficiency in swimming, with reference to saving life from drowning. Local humane societies were also established, several of which awarded medals, including those at Northampton in 1789, Glasgow in 1790, Bristol in 1807 and Liverpool in 1831.

The Royal National Lifeboat Institution Medal was awarded to those who displayed exceptional bravery in saving or attempting to save life in shipwrecks on the coasts of the United Kingdom. It was awarded in gold or silver, and sometimes occurs with an elaborate suspension loop. Their first medal, by W. Wyon, has a portrait of its patron George IV (*obv.*) and is dated 1824 (**266**), the year of its foundation. The bust of Queen Victoria (*obv.*) is on the next issue, by L.C. Wyon, dated 1860. A standard reverse illustrates three men in a boat, one of whom pulls a survivor from water. Those subsequently awarded carried a new reverse.

The Board of Trade instituted a medal, awarded in silver or bronze from 1855, to those who risked their own lives, or who were indirectly responsible for the saving of life: with a bust of Queen Victoria (*obv.*), and survivors on a raft in rough seas, awaiting an approaching lifeboat (*rev.*), by B. Wyon. In 1905, a smaller version of these medals was introduced.

The East Indiaman, *Kent*, which caught fire in the Bay of Biscay in 1825, is recalled on a medal by T. Halliday, presented in silver to those who participated in the rescue (when, by good fortune, a ship nearby managed to despatch a boat, thus saving many lives). Survivors from a burning ship are rescued by a boat (*obv.*), with the inscription 'to commemorate the destruction of the Kent East Indiaman by fire . . . 547 persons, thus providentially delivered from death' (*rev.*). Examples in bronze and white metal were sold as souvenirs.

The Royal Geographical Society has awarded several medals, the earliest of which is their Founder's Medal, with a bust of William IV (*obv.*), and Britannia standing beside a sextant and globe (*rev.*), by W. Wyon. It was awarded annually in gold from 1839–1974, and thereafter in gilt silver, for the encouragement of geographical science and discovery. In 1874, the Society instigated a medal by A.B. Wyon to be awarded in silver to those who had transported the body of David Livingstone, who had died in 1873, from Ilala in central Africa to the coast: with his bust (*obv.*), and the inscription 'presented by the Royal Geographical Society of London 1874' (*rev.*) (**267**), with the recipient's name inscribed on the edge, followed by 'faithful to the end'. Henry Morton Stanley's expedition in 1887–9 to rescue Emin Pasha is commemorated on a large cast medal dated 1890, presented by the Society, but not inscribed, to members of the expedition and to the families of those who had died. It carries a fine portrait of Stanley (*obv.*), and a seated figure of Africa emptying waters of the Congo and Nile (*rev.*), by E. Hallé. Captain Scott's Antarctic expedition of 1902–4 was the subject of a medal by G. Bayes which the Royal Geographical Society presented in gold and silver to Scott and his crew, respectively: with a bust of Scott (*obv.*), and the team and their ship *Discovery* (*rev.*). A somewhat similar medal by Bayes was presented, again in gold and silver, to Ernest Shackleton, the commander of an Antarctic expedition in 1909. The Society's medal, by F. Bowcher, for Scott's ill-fated Antarctic expedition in 1910–13 was presented to the officers and scientific staff in silver, and to the crew in bronze: with Scott's bust (*obv.*), and the expedition advancing with skis and sledge (*rev.*).

The first flight over Mount Everest in 1933 is commemorated on an interesting medal by P. Metcalfe, with a biplane in flight and mountains beyond (*obv.*), and a presentation inscription (*rev.*) (**268**). It was commissioned by *The Times*, which had decided at the eleventh hour to award a medal to members of the expedition. In order to minimise any risk to the dies on striking (there being little time to prepare another pair), the metal blanks were made of pure silver instead of the customary, and slightly harder, sterling .925 fineness. The entire project, from its conception to striking, took just two weeks.

Medals given for encouragement, or to honour an achievement, are usually named when awarded. They can, however, also take the form of honorary or diplomatic presentations, which usually do not have an added engraved inscription. In the nineteenth century, silver medals were struck by the Royal Mint for presentation to British and foreign royalty making official visits to the Mint. Frequent use was made of a crown die with which to strike the obverse, while an appropriate inscription recording the visit was simply placed on the reverse, obviating the need for a special design. The medals could thus be struck at very little notice, while having an official and distinctive flavour. Prince George of Cumberland's visit in 1828, one of the first to be so marked, employs W. Wyon's obverse die for the 1825 pattern crown (**269**). A succession of visits during the nineteenth century are commemorated by similar medals, such as the Duke of York's in 1894, the obverse this time provided by T. Brock's 'veiled head' Victorian crown.

Since the eighteenth century, the British Government has presented medals to North American Indian chiefs, as tokens of friendship, rewards for loyalty, and to signify the conclusion of treaties. They do not comprise a uniform series, although all carry the sovereign's portrait and often have a suspension loop so that they can be worn. These medals represented gestures of a very personal kind and they were highly regarded mementoes, proudly worn by the recipients, as can be seen on some paintings. The earliest issues, those from the reign of George I, are undated and somewhat coarsely made, with the bust of 'George King of Britain' (*obv.*), and an Indian firing an arrow at a deer (*rev.*). They, and those of similar style from the early part of George II's reign, were struck in brass. Another George II issue dated 1757 has an Indian being offered a pipe by a European settler (*rev.*); this medal was made of silver, as were all subsequent medals. Several different types were made during the reign of George III: the two most common carry the King's portrait (*obv.*), and the royal coat of arms and supporters (*rev.*). The first was issued *c.* 1770 and occurs in various sizes, and is in both a completely struck and hollow form. The other standard issue, by T. Wyon Jr, dated 1814, was struck in three sizes (**80**). During the 1870s treaties were negotiated and concluded with various chiefs in Canada, for which medals were presented: with a bust of Victoria (*obv.*), and the Canadian Treaty Commissioner and an Indian shaking hands, the date and number of the treaty added to an otherwise plain border (*rev.*) (**270**), by J.S. and A.B. Wyon.

Various medals have been given to and inscribed with the names of commodity brokers and members of the various companies within the City of London. From *c.* 1707, silver medals were presented by the Corporation of London to each sworn licensed broker in stocks or other commodities, to be produced if a client, before transacting business, wished to see some *bona fide* evidence of their status. The medals consisted of the Royal coat of arms and motto (*obv.*), and those of the City of London, with a panel for the holder's name (*rev.*) (**271**). This design remained largely unchanged throughout the different issues of this medal, the need for which ceased in the 1880s. Since the mid eighteenth century, medals of more than forty City of London companies have been made, usually consisting of the company's coat of arms (*obv.*), and an engraved inscription of the holder's name and the date of admission to the Company (*rev.*). These include those of the Apothecaries', Brasiers', Carpenters', Cooks', Distillers', Fishmongers', Needlemakers', Tylers' (**272**) and Vintners' Companies.

Chapter 5

Collecting medals today

However much the science of medals has developed over the past 300 years, embracing an intellectually wide circle of people, the subject is still wide open to discovery. In many cases, the most pertinent questions which can be asked – Who made the medal and why? Who was it made for and how was it distributed? – remain unanswered. The study of one particular aspect or theme is usually the most rewarding. In much the same way, a group or a collection of medals confined to a single topic is of greater interest than the sum of its individual parts (*see* **Plates 35–6**).

A great deal of literature has been devoted to various aspects of the subject over the last twenty-five years. Philip Attwood's 'The Society of Medallists' (*The Medal* 3, 1983, pp. 4–11) brings to light an important but little-known school of medal-makers; Peter Barbers' *Diplomacy – the world of the Honest Spy* (London, 1972) places the medal in a fascinating historical context; Graham Dyer's 'Thomas Humphrey Paget (1893–1974)' *NC* 1980 pp. 165–77, lucidly discusses a medallist's career in a Mint context; Mark Jones' 'The Medal as an Instrument of Propaganda in late 17th and early 18th Century Europe' (*NC* 1982, pp. 117–26; 1983 pp. 202–13), discusses the causes and the purpose of these medals, and interprets their inscriptions and imagery; Graham Pollard's 'Matthew Boulton and Conrad Heinrich Küchler' (*NC* 1970, pp. 259–318) is a pioneer study on a major series; Thomas Stainton's 'John Milton, medallist, 1759–1805', (*BNJ* 1983, pp. 133–59) is a meticulous investigation of a medallist's work. This is only a small selection of the many books and papers which have been written on medals, although related aspects, such as preparatory sketches, models, moulds and dies, have not, as yet, received the same attention. Museums, numismatic libraries, Mint records, societies with original documents, private diaries, and public archives such as the Public Record Office, all contain documentary sources of information.

Public collections in Britain include those at the Ashmolean Museum (Oxford), Birmingham Museum and Art Gallery, British Museum, Fitzwilliam Museum (Cambridge), Hunterian Museum (Glasgow), Museum of London, National Army Museum (London), National Maritime Museum (London), National Museum of Antiquities (Edinburgh), and the Victoria and Albert Museum (London); the latter, with an outstanding group of Renaissance and later medals on permanent display.

94

There is also a good collection in the National Museum of Ireland (Dublin). The British Museum has probably the most diverse, if not the largest, collection of medals in the world, a source frequently drawn upon for exhibitions and publications. Since its foundation in 1753, it has maintained close links with the subject. In addition, many provincial museums have collections relating to a locality or theme, to which some curators pay a great deal of interest. Regrettably, most public medal collections are not on permanent display and an appointment to view is therefore necessary.

The Royal Mint in Llantrisant (South Wales) has its own curatorial staff and private museum, which includes a reference collection of medals, particularly strong in those made since 1816 by the Mint itself. However, its true distinction is that it contains many of the actual dies used for striking, one of the oldest of which is for the reverse of Thomas Simon's coronation medal of Charles II (*see* **fig. 2**). These items are not usually available to the general public, but access can be arranged for serious students. From 1870 to 1977, records of Royal Mint production were documented in published annual reports and these include information of the medals struck, quantities produced, distribution, purity of metals, as well as other relevant nuggets of information.

The British Art Medal Society, founded in 1982, is the only organization in the United Kingdom devoted exclusively to the study of medals and the encouragement of medallic art. It issues a twice-yearly journal, *The Medal*, which contains important articles on the subject and current news and views, the standards of which have already earned it an international reputation. The Society arranges a programme of monthly winter meetings in London, and an annual Spring conference with lectures, exhibits, a medal workshop, and other activities. Details of membership can be obtained from the British Museum, c/o Department of Coins and Medals, Great Russell St, London WC1B 3DG.

Most of the numismatic societies in Britain belong to the British Association of Numismatic Societies (BANS), which holds an annual congress. They all cater for a wide range of numismatic interests, but with an emphasis on coins, and hold a programme of monthly meetings at which papers are read. The published proceedings, in annual volumes, of the British Numismatic Society's (Warburg Institute, Woburn Square, London WC1) *British Numismatic Journal*, and the Royal Numismatic Society's (Society of Antiquaries, Burlington House, Piccadilly, London W1C 0HS) *Numismatic Chronicle* contain significant papers on British medals, a few of which have already been mentioned. Members of both societies have the facilities of a joint library which contains many books on medals. Details of all numismatic societies can be obtained from the British Museum, c/o Department of Coins and Medals.

Coin News is a monthly magazine which includes some coverage of medals, as well as details of events in the numismatic world. Magazines such as *The Antique Collector, Apollo,* and *The Burlington* sometimes include articles on medals, usually in an art-history context.

Several countries have thriving medal-making industries, as well as active societies concerned with their study, including Belgium, Finland, France, Germany (Federal Republic), Holland, Portugal, Sweden and the U.S.A. Many are members of FIDEM (Fédération Internationale de la Médaille), which organizes an international biennial conference, where recent medallic work is shown, and for which a catalogue of the proceedings is published. Details can be obtained either from the British Museum's Department of Coins and Medals or from the Secretariat General, 6, place Saint-Germain-des-Près, 75006 Paris, France.

Only towards the end of the nineteenth century were medal exhibitions mounted with any degree of frequency, at the British Museum in 1881 and 1891, and by the Society of Medallists at South Kensington in 1885. The Universal Exposition in Paris in 1900 contained contemporary medals. So too did that organized in New York in 1910 by the American Numismatic Society, which showed the work of many leading European and American medallists. Forty-two countries participated at the 1951 international exposition in Madrid, for which the Royal Mint submitted medals and seals. The 'Medals Today' exhibition held in 1973 at the Goldsmiths' Hall, London, consisted exclusively of medals by contemporary artists. The exhibition held at the British Museum in 1979, 'The Medal, Mirror of History', has been perhaps the most wide-ranging, providing an excellent overview of the subject. In 1987–88, the American Numismatic Society organized an exhibition in New York of almost 400 medals, 'The Beaux-Arts Medal in America', covering the years *c.* 1880–1920.

The cycle of buying and selling between private collectors, museums, dealers and auctioneers, has been going on for more than 200 years. The London auction houses of Christie's, Glendining's, Sotheby's and Spink's regularly hold sales of medals, sometimes together with coins, for which they issue a catalogue. Before each auction, lots can be examined at appointed viewing times. A great deal of work goes into the preparation of these catalogues, and they often remain as useful sources of reference long after the auction has taken place. In addition, they can provide the provenance of a particular medal, thereby giving it an added appeal, and a pointer towards what was then available and in vogue.

Examples of the many medal collections which have been dispersed over the years include those of Oppenheimer (Renaissance) 1936, and O'Byrne (British and European) 1962, by Christie's; Farquhar (British) 1955, and Swan (railways) 1986, by Glendining's; Heckett (British) 1977, and the Duke of Northumberland (European) 1980–81, by Sotheby's; European 1980, and Italian Baroque 1981, both anonymous, by Spink's. Among the greatest private collections of general British medals to have

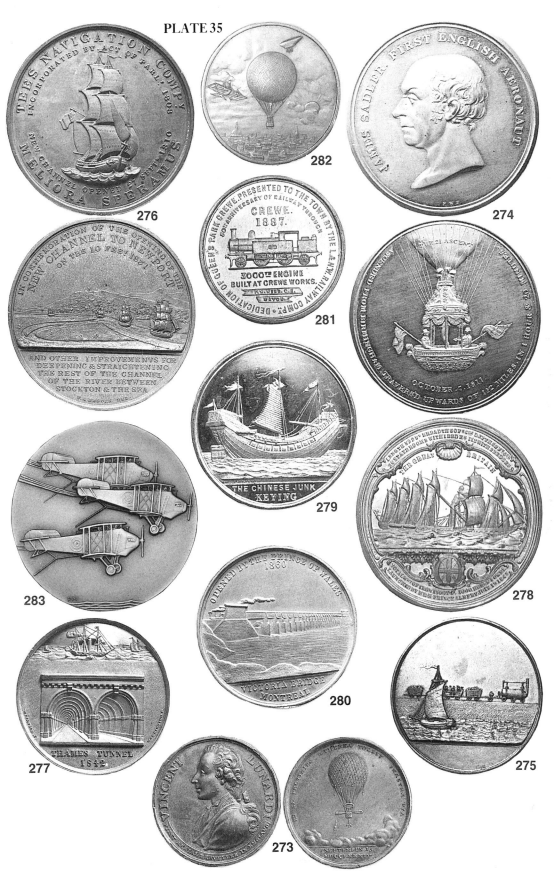

PLATE 35

284   285   286   287   288

289   290   291

PLATE 36

293   292   295

296   294   298

299   297   300

been sold (by Sotheby's) were those of Hyman Montagu, in 1897, containing over 800 lots, some with multiple medals, and John G. Murdoch, in 1904, equally large, but with different emphases. Remarkable medals fetched remarkable prices at both auctions, and it is unlikely that similar private collections could be formed today.

Many coin dealers maintain medals as part of their general stock, as do sometimes general antique dealers. The specialist medal dealer, of whom there is only a small number, will usually be able to offer a greater degree of guidance as well as, of course, a larger selection of medals for sale. The British Numismatic Trade Association issues a free list containing names and addresses of its members, among which are several medal dealers, and organizes an annual fair in the autumn, where medals can be bought and sold. Details can be obtained from The Secretary, BNTA Ltd, P.O. Box 82, Coventry CV5 6RS. The International Association of Professional Numismatists has several member-dealers who handle medals; they too issue a list of their members, which can be obtained from The Secretariat, IAPN, 11 Adelphi Terrace, London WC2N 6BJ.

Contemporary medals are available from a number of sources. The British Art Medal Society commissions original medallic work, notices of which appear in its journal *The Medal*. Each medal is available to members for a limited period, after which time the issue is closed. Commemorative medals produced by the Royal Mint can be purchased as and when they come out, either directly through the Royal Mint Club (P.O. Box 500, Cardiff, CF1 1HA) which issues a quarterly magazine, or from the Mint's agents. A number of private mints are today producing medals, such as the Tower Mint, whose medals are sold as mementoes at historic castles and houses.

Dealers' lists and auction catalogues are ways of establishing approximate and comparative prices, although the factor of demand, at times irrational, can make a considerable difference. A medal in its original case and condition will command a premium, as will one which retains an original gilding. Cast medals are most desirable if they are contemporary, display clean and tidy fields and lettering, and are pleasantly patinated. When a prize medal has been awarded, usually by means of an engraved inscription, it fulfills its intended function and is of greater interest than if unissued. The difference which this can make to value is influenced by its subject-matter, the status of the recipient, and the part played in gaining the award. There are instances when it makes little or no difference, but others when the value can be increased by a factor of five or even ten.

Comparisons are never really conclusive, although weight of opinion does suggest that compared with coins, campaign medals and other commemoratives such as ceramics, the current prices of medals are low, and perhaps ridiculously so. On the face of it, this is surprising, bearing in mind their qualities and the long history of interest in the subject. However, being considered by a wider public as merely an adjunct to coins, or being confused with campaign medals, has hardly allowed medals to establish their own identity. At the same time, their comparative rarity prevents a wider availability and, therefore, better understanding of the subject. On occasion, however, the factor of scarcity can become a two-edged sword, when demand can push prices to unexpected heights. At a London auction in 1988 of contemporary paintings, drawings and sculpture, Lynn Chadwick's 'Diamond Head' (**126**) sold for £450, having been available to members of the British Art Medal Society in 1984 for £25. While this does not suggest what another example might fetch, it does illustrate how, on some occasions, and when placed in a different context, medal prices can be unpredictable. An approximate guide to prices which a collector might reasonably expect to pay accompanies the list of illustrations after the Glossary, although they cannot allow for the caprices of an erratic or sensitive market. .

Most medals have been privately made in quantities which have not usually been recorded. Generally, only a minority of medals have been made in tens or, very occasionally, in hundreds of thousands; while most have been produced in the hundreds, and for some less than one hundred is a likely figure. Many collectors seem to be obsessed with rarity, the investment platform upon which medals were marketed during the 1960s and 70s, but with disappointment for the buyers. On the other hand, time has shown that the building of a medal collection over a number of years can be an effective way of creating an investment. However, invariably, this is achieved when only interest and pleasure are the motivating forces. After all, every medal tells a different story, regardless of how common or otherwise, and rarity alone does not govern interest or value.

A medal in an excellent state of preservation is not only more pleasing to look at than an inferior example, but will, market forces dictating, fetch a greater price, whichever side of the counter you are standing. This may not unduly concern a collector with an interest in a specific subject, where the illustration of a theme may be of greater importance than the medal's overall appearance. It may also be true that a particular medal does not frequently appear, and the choice then has to be made, whether to obtain an inferior example or wait for a better one. However, as a general rule, rather one good medal than ten mediocre!

A relative scale of terms (fine, very fine, extremely fine) is used to describe the overall condition of a medal. There are, however, particular points to look out for when assessing condition. The weight and the relief of many medals make them susceptible to knocks on the edge, nicks and scratches in the field, and friction on the highest points of the portrait and design: damage which is characteristic of a medal having been dropped, rubbed against another, or cleaned. Cleaning can damage the surface and will often remove a fine, sometimes centuries-old, patina, replacing it with an unsightly shine and numerous hair-line scratches. For some curious reason, the cleaning both of medals and of silver household objects is commonly, but mistakenly, thought of as equally appropriate. Natural toning and patination on medals is usually very pleasant, and certainly preferred to a bright and artificial 'gloss'. The cleaning of medals is therefore not recommended, except to remove, with a dry and very soft brush, particles of loose dirt or dust which do accumulate in the design and lettering. Handling medals by the edge will help to avoid surface marks, which dirt or sweat promote.

Distinguishing between an original or contemporary cast, and a later or 'after-cast' is, to a great extent, a matter of experience. Looking at and comparing examples of cast medals, with an eye to certain criteria, as outlined in the Glossary, will enable the differences to become clearer. Electrotypes and restrikes are discussed in the Glossary but, generally speaking, medals have not been subject to outright forgery.

Fitted cases for medals date back to the seventeenth century, at which time they were usually circular and often made of shagreen, an untanned leather prepared from the skin of a shark or seal. The interiors were usually lined with velvet, the lids secured by means of metal hinges and sliding hooks. More usual are square or circular cases in leather, box-wood, or card, which date back to the late eighteenth century, and sometimes carry details of the publisher or engraver on the inside lining of the lid. They might also include a pamphlet or poster with information about the medal or the circumstances of its issue. The English version of the *Lusitania* medal, together with a poster relating to its sinking in 1915, was contained in a cardboard case with an illustration of the ship on the outside lid. Corporation of London medals were often issued in fitted cases with commentaries of the event inscribed in gilt lettering on the outside lid.

For permanent display, a wall-mounted cabinet lined with material such as hessian can provide both a suitable housing and an effective backdrop, the medals themselves held in position by mapping pins; this method is employed at museums. A wooden cabinet is a traditional means of housing medals, although it prevents their immediate viewing. They date back to the seventeenth and eighteenth centuries and can be attractive pieces of furniture, some being made by famous cabinet-makers, examples of which can be seen in museums. Cabinets from the nineteenth century and later can sometimes be bought for reasonable sums at dealers and auctions, while a well-made modern cabinet can often cost as much. These methods of display, indeed any involving medals at home, carry some degree of risk, one which is unavoidable if they are to be readily available. An alternative is the deposit of the collection in a bank, while a photographic or written record of each medal can be kept at home. This will provide a certain degree of security, and itself may form the basis of a catalogue.

I hope that the pleasure and inspiration which medals can offer have been brought to light in this Introduction and that the reader will be spurred on to find out more. I have found medals to be a fascinating source of information, in many ways quite unique. They can convey much of the past, embodying as they do, the art and history of their times. They can be many things to different people: historical records, a gallery of portraits or simply works of art. Whatever, they provide a rich, but undervalued vein to be tapped, one that may surprise but never disappoint.

Glossary

Annealing: softening of metal by exposure to a continuous and slowly diminished heat.

Anon(ymous): an unsigned medal and one which cannot be attributed to a medallist.

Blanching: removal of copper from the surface of silver-copper alloys in order to obtain the whiteness of a purer silver coat.

Blank: piece of plain metal upon which an impression is made when struck with a die.

Calendar: in 1582, Pope Gregory XIII introduced a 'New Style' calendar (the Gregorian) in order to rectify the errors of that introduced by Julius Caesar (the Julian) in 45 BC. The Gregorian calendar conformed more closely to the natural courses of the seasons and made the year correspond as nearly as possible to the true solar year. The Julian year, or 'Old Style', of 365¼ days, allowing for any leap years, resulted in an annual difference between the two of 11 minutes and 10 seconds. By the time Britain wished to adopt the 'New Style' in 1752 (most European countries had made the change within twenty years of its introduction), its calendar had become eleven days out of sequence. In order to correct the discrepancy, 2 September was in that year followed by 14 September. The dates on some medals made before 1752 will not, therefore, always concur precisely with the event commemorated; for example **25** and **32**.

Cameography: a less well known and little used process for the manufacture of medals, developed by Henry M. Edmunds in 1923. Series of fine parallel lines are engraved upon a sheet of plate glass and projected by a powerful lantern on the face of the sitter, who is then photographed from two points. The negatives show the image of the person and the fine lines across the face, which naturally appear as curved lines where they fall across the features. The plates are then enlarged to a particular size on glass transparencies and placed in a specially constructed carving machine in which several hundred parallel furrows are carved by a revolving drill, controlled by the contour lines registered on the plate. The result is a portrait in relief, which shows a remarkable life-like appearance. A small number of medals were made by the Cameograph Co. in the 1920s.

Casting: one of the two primary methods of medal making (*see* **Striking**) which can take two forms. A model of the proposed medal is made, from which a mould is taken; extra definition, if required, is then added to the mould. When another mould has been made for the reverse (assuming a medal with two sides), the two are joined together and molten metal poured in through a conveniently-placed recess. Sometimes the two sides of a medal are cast separately and then joined together by their edges.

In the second procedure, known as the *cire perdue*, or 'lost-wax' process, a completed model in wax is tightly clad in moulding material, which takes an impression of the model. The outside casing is then heated and the wax (from the model) runs out of a recess provided. This is then replaced by molten metal, which fills the mould which the model created.

There are several variations in the procedures for casting: in the materials used to make the models, which were often wax, or less commonly of wood or stone; in the preparation of the moulds; in the tooling and chasing in the fields in order to emphasize relief design; in the drawing of the lettering on the mould or on the finished medal; and in the methods of patination, whereby a medallist might apply a lacquer or varnish. The skill of the medallist in arranging the composition of the metals, usually copper or lead, and fixing the temperature at which the medal was to be cast, was very often revealed in the texture of the medal's surface. The finished medal could be retouched with an engraving tool in order to remove air-bubbles or other defects, which had occurred during casting, such as those created by sand or other materials used to line the mould. Ultimately, all these techniques depended largely upon the medallist, and the school to which he or she belonged.

Medals which have not been cast from an original mould, but from one made by an already existing medal, an 'after-cast', will probably shrink to some degree. One method of determining the originality of a cast medal is to measure its diameter. However, as some medallists 'finished' their cast by filing the edges to remove roughness, a more reliable measurement is that taken from two fixed points within the medal and not from the edge. Some medallists placed two circular lines on their original models to serve as a guide for the placement of lettering. These lines are usually visible on a medal which is an original or an early cast, and appear as two fine circular grooves faithfully tracing the sweep of the inscriptions.

This is only a brief sketch of the two processes. A more thorough discussion can be found in Hill/Pollard and Dutton (*see* Bibliography) which describe techniques used by craftsmen in the Renaissance and those employed by a living medallist, respectively.

Chronogrammatic date: (the incorporation of) a date in the inscription, whereby Roman-numeral letters are enlarged and provide a date when added, as in: I LIke MeDaLs $= 1+50+1+1000+500+50 = 1602$.

Cliché: a uniface striking on a wafer-thin blank, the clear impression of which is also visible, in 'negative', on the reverse.

Collar: device in which the blank is positioned, when struck with a die, to prevent the metal from spreading, thereby ensuring a perfectly round medal.

Copies: *see* **Cast, Electrotype** *and* **Restrike**.

Dates: most medals were made at the time of the date shown or within a few years of it, but not all by any means. For example, both the cutting of dies and the striking of a medal may have occurred some years later than that suggested by its date.

On the other hand, dies for a proposed medal may have been cut at a particular time and for a particular event but, for whatever reason, only actually used many years later. (*See also* **Calendar, Chronogrammatic** *and* **Roman numerals**).

Diadem: type of open, small crown.

Die: metal, often of steel, on which a design is engraved in 'negative' (*see* **fig. 2**). When struck on a metal blank, it creates that design in 'positive'. Die-cutting was carried out with special engravers' tools; often a slow and tedious process, requiring the highest skills of engraving. Impressions taken in material, such as clay or plasticine, enabled the engraver to create sample strikings and examine the progress. On completion of the cutting, the die would need to be hardened and given protection from the actions of fire and water. It is covered with an oil-based paste and powdered animal charcoal, heated to a precise temperature, depending upon the chemical properties of the steel used to make the die, and then plunged into cold water. (*See also* **Striking**).

Die flaws: a medal exhibiting flaws in the metal may have been struck from a cracked die. The die's state of deterioration will be reflected on the medal.

Edges: these are usually plain. Seventeenth and eighteenth-century medals are those most likely to have lettered edges.

Electrotyping: a process developed in the 1830s which was an electrical equivalent of metal casting. An artist's design in wax was put into a specially prepared wax mould, from which was taken a wax impression treated with powdered graphite. Copper conductor pegs were inserted into the back of the wax and the whole was then immersed in a solution into which an electric current was introduced, connected from a battery via the wax to a copper sheet. The current would dissolve copper from the sheet, which would form a fine deposition on the surface of the wax impression. When the process was complete, the wax could be removed from the thin copper plate now formed. Two similarly made shells with packing material sandwiched between could be joined at their edges to form a complete medal.

Electrotype medals will usually display tell-tale signs such as a thin line running around the edge, at the point where the two halves have been joined. Another characteristic of electrotype medals is that when 'rung' by another piece of metal, they will usually emit a muted or dead sound, unlike cast or struck medals which will, unless made of lead, emit a clear 'ping'. A combination of factors should be sufficient to detect an electrotype. The process has been used to copy celebrated medals, particularly those of great rarity. It has also been used to produce medals whose large size and complexity of design may have posed problems in the preparation and striking of a die.

Engraving: design and lettering cut into the surface by means of an engraving tool. The technique of engraving a design or portrait on to metal achieved considerable heights in the early seventeenth century. One of the most celebrated practitioners was Simon de Passe who engraved, on thin oval silver and gold plates, Tudor and Stuart portraits with the three-dimensional qualities of a miniature. During the eighteenth and nineteenth centuries, regimental, shooting and academic silver medals were frequently engraved and hall-marked.

Exergue: an area of the medal, usually separated by a horizontal line, situated in the bottom portion of the design. It sometimes contains a date or an inscription.

Extremely fine: a state of preservation, whereby the medal retains much of its original colour, shows little signs of wear, and only the slightest hint of having been handled. A medal which is in a particularly fine state of preservation might be regarded as good extremely fine. (*See* **Very fine**.)

Field: the plain background area of the medal.

Frosted: with a fine white matt finish (which looks somewhat like icing on a cake). It was often applied to prize medals of the nineteenth century, which were set within two watch-style glasses framed with a silver band. (*See also* **Glass cases**.)

Garter: a decorative device in the form of a belt, often inscribed 'Honi. Soit. Qui. Mal. Y. Pense.'

Glass cases: prize and society medals were often set within two watch-style glasses or 'lunettes', and framed with a silver band. A practice beginning at the end of the eighteenth century and lasting about 100 years. (*See also* **Frosted**.)

Guinea: the term for a sum of 21 shillings or £1 1s., expressed in today's terms as £1.05p. It is also a term for an old gold coin of that value, the last of which is dated 1813.

Gutta-percha: gum consisting of the thickened and condensed juice from the Malayan percha tree, first used *c.* 1845.

Incuse: (lettering or design) sunk into the surface of the medal. (*See also* **Relief**.)

Inscriptions: Those in Latin commonly use certain forms of letters, such as I and V in place of J and U. The following Latin words, together with their commonly-abbreviated forms, are among those which occur on medals:

ANG(LIA)	England	FID(EI)	faith
AVSP(ICES)	guidance/patronage	FRA	France
BRIT(AN)	Britain	GEOR(GIVS)	George
CAR(OLVS)	Charles	G(RATIA)	grace
COM(ES)	Earl	GUIL(IELMVS)	William
CORON(AT)	coronation	HIB(ERNIA)	Ireland
D(EI)	God	IAC(OBVS)	James
DVX	duke	IMP(ERATOR)	emperor
ET	and	IOH(ANNES)	John

MAG(NA)	great	PAT(RIA)	country
MAR(IA)	Mary	PRIN(CEPS)	prince
NAT(VS)	born	REG/REX	queen/king
NVPT(IA)	marriage	SOC(IETAS)	society
OB(IIT)	died	SPES	hope
PACE/PAX	peace	WALLIAE	Wales
PAT(ER)	father		

Intaglio: design or lettering that has been cut in 'negative' on a die, and which produces, when struck, a 'positive' image in relief.

Legends: *see* **Inscriptions**.

Lunettes: *see* **Glass cases**.

Measurements: diameters and weights are usually and most practically stated in millimetres and grammes.

Medallist: in the context of this work, a person involved in the making or issue of medals: i.e. an engraver, designer, die-sinker, editor, jeweller, publisher, sculptor, silversmith, etc., and not someone who has been awarded a medal. Some medals are signed not only by the engraver but also by a die-sinker or publisher. The signature on a medal struck from a worn die is often one of the first features to become indistinct.

New Style: *see* **Calendar**.

Obverse: the premier side of the medal on which appears the principal design, such as a portrait. Hence the expression, 'heads' for the obverse of a tossed coin, and 'tails' for the reverse, which it normally complements.

Old Style: *see* **Calendar**.

Pinchbeck: an alloy of about five parts copper with one of zinc, with characteristics of brass. First used in the 1730s for clock-making, in cheap jewellery, and for medals.

Presentation or **prize medals**: usually have an engraved inscription of name and date, when they are awarded. Medals were normally awarded in certain metals; those otherwise made are usually 'proof' or 'specimen' strikings by the medallist, possibly for sale to the public as souvenirs of the event. The terms governing the award of a prize medal can change, such as its frequency and the metal in which it is presented. A standard obverse was sometimes used, but with more than one reverse.

Reducing machine: three-dimensional pantograph which produces a master punch in relief from an electrotype copy of the artist's plaster model. Its introduction in the 1820s offered the potential of simplifying the preparation of the die, which no longer had to be directly engraved by hand. The medallist could now work out the design in wax, or in a similar material, on a large scale. From this advanced model, a simple mould could be made, in turn providing a plaster cast on which the medallist could perfect the design (*see* **fig. 15**). An iron casting could then be made and the actual size required for the final work would be produced by means of the reducing machine.

Relief: lettering or design which is above the field, as is the case with the overwhelming majority of medals. (*See also* **Incuse**).

Repoussé: hammered or worked into relief from the reverse side of a metal plate. Two such pieces could then be joined at their edges to constitute a complete medal, with extra chasing and ornamentation added, if required. Sometimes the hollow centre between the two plates was filled with a ballast to give the medal substance. Through the process of manufacture, a small hole occurs in the metal. The technique was practised during the seventeenth century by Dutch medallists. Cast versions of repoussé medals were made, both contemporaneously and later.

Restrikes: the Royal Mint does not have a tradition for restriking their commemorative medals. The Mints of France and the United States have restruck medals from original or slightly altered dies. Since 1832 many French medals have a tiny symbol impressed on the edge, such as an antique lamp, anchor or cornucopia, from which can be determined the date of manufacture. Restrikes can sometimes be distinguished by a light, almost-green, matt patina. Some medals are restruck from old dies which, in the passage of time, have become rusty. Such defects will usually show up on the medal as pimples and flaws.

Reverse: the 'other' side of the *obverse*, which it normally complements, and to which it is usually secondary.

Roman numerals: usually occur in a conventional or a chronogrammatic form. A less common arrangement occurs as letters which need to be joined. An example is CIƆIƆCCIIX, whereon the first three letters are linked to form an M, and the following two a D. When followed by the remaining letters, the date of MDCCIIX (1708) is formed.

Screw-press: *see* **Striking**.

Striking: the other primary process (*see* **Casting**), whereby the medal is formed by the striking of a die upon a metal blank, reproducing its design and lettering and, thus, the medal. Medals were first struck in the early sixteenth century by means of a screw-press, whereby the two dies (assuming a medal with two sides) were positioned vertically and securely, in between which was the metal blank. The arms of the press were then turned, sending the upper punch downwards. This would strike the metal blank, which now would also receive an impression from the lower die.

The design of a medal in high relief could not always be impressed by a single blow of the die. The blank would therefore be removed, annealed for softening, and exactly fitted for a second blow; in cases of exceptional relief, several blows would be necessary to obtain the whole design. This is a very simplified account of striking, the technical aspects of which are more fully outlined in *The Art and Craft of Coinmaking, A History of Minting Technology* by Denis R. Cooper, London, 1988. (*See also* **Die**.)

Tombac: an alloy of copper and zinc in various proportions, sometimes referred to as Mannheim gold or Prince's metal. Developed in the early seventeenth century, but used in medals, infrequently, in the 1930s.

Truncation: the line of the head or bust where it is cut off from the rest of the body. Here is sometimes found a date or a medallist's name or initials.

Uniface: (medal with) a design and lettering on one side only.

Very fine: a state of preservation whereby a medal, although not still in the first flush of youth, retains a little of its original colour and has only a modest amount of wear on the high points. A medal which has rather a lot of wear may be referred to as being in fine condition. (*See also* **Extremely fine**).

Abbreviations

Al	aluminium
AE	bronze or copper
AR	silver
AV	gold
BL	British Library
c.	circa (or about, with reference to dates)
EF	extremely fine
ex.	exergue
F	fine
Fe.	iron
fl.	flourished
inscr.	inscription
l.	left
mm.	millimetres
obv.	obverse
Pb	lead
PRO	Public Record Office
Pt	platinum
r.	right
rev.	reverse
trans.	translated
VF	very fine
WM	white metal

Monetary conversion

6d (six pence)	= 2½p
1s. (one shilling)	= 5p
20s. (twenty shillings)	= £1
1 guinea (21 shillings)	= £1.05

Illustrated medals and their values

Values are for medals in extremely fine (EF) condition, except nos. 1–22, 34–5, 39, 80, 136, 150, 157, 181, 184–6, 194, 245, and 271a, which are priced in very fine (VF). Medals in a particularly fine state of preservation (good EF) will command a premium. A few rare or otherwise unavailable medals are left unpriced. The values apply to medals which are attractive and uncleaned examples, without nicks, scratches, edge knocks or other defects, except those of the most minor nature. Cast medals should be those which are original and with attractive patination. The values are intended only as an approximate and comparative guide as to what a collector might expect to pay.

Non-circular medals have their width stated first. When only one side of a medal has been illustrated on the plate and described in the text, a brief description is given of the other. Medals are struck, unless otherwise indicated.

*Commissioned and sold by the British Art Medal Society to its members for £22 (contents page, 122, 124, 130); £25 (126, 129, 131–2, 134); and £30 (133).

	Plate 1	£
1	Pisanello: Leonello d'Este, *c.* 1444. Cast, 67 mm.	*AE* 7000
2	Pasti: Isote degli Atti, 1446. Cast, 84 mm. (photo: J. Schulman B.V.)	*AE* 3000
3	Pasti: Sigismondo Malatesta, 1450. Cast, 40 mm.	*AE* 700
4	Enzola: Francesco I Sforza, 1475. Cast, 43 mm.	*AE* 400

	Plate 2	
5	Enzola: Constanzo Sforza, 1475. Cast, 81 mm.	*AE* 3000
6	Pisanello: John Paleologus, *c.* 1438. Cast, 104 mm. (*obv.* Paleologus)	*AE* —— *Pb* ——
7	Torre: Marcantonio Flaminio, *c.*1530. Cast, 67 mm.	*AE* 3000
8	Pastorino: Ludovico Ariosto, *c.* 1550. Cast, 38 mm.	*AE* 400

	Plate 3	
9	Pastorino: Alfonso II d'Este, *c.* 1560. Cast, 60 mm.	*Pb* 400
10	Abondio: Maximilian II, *c.* 1575. Cast, 59 mm. (*rev.* plain)	*AR* 1200

£

11 Galeotti: Giambatista Castaldi, *c.* 1550. Cast, 46 mm.   *AE* 2500
12 Leoni: Andrea Doria, *c.* 1540. Cast, 42 mm.   *AE* 500
13 Trezzo: Mary I of England, 1555. Cast, 68 mm.   *AR* 1800
  AE 600
14 Le Clerc: Anne of Britanny, 1499. Cast, 114 mm.   *AE* 2500
  (*obv.* Louis XII)

Plate 4
15 Gebel: Albrecht Dürer, 1528. Cast, 39 mm. (*rev.* inscr.)   *Pb* 300
16 Reinhart: Johann Friedrich of Saxony, 1535. Cast,   *AR* 1500
  66 mm.
17 Maler: Sebalt Haller, 1569. Cast, 60 mm. (*rev.* Andreas   *AR* 800
  Imhof)
18 Matsys: William Schevez, 1491. Cast, 79 mm.   *AE* ——
  (*rev.* armorial shield)
19 Herwick: Maria Dimock, 1562. Cast, 40 mm.   *AR* 600
  (*rev.* female and stag)
20 Jonghelinck: Margaret of Parma, 1567. Cast, 58 mm.   *AR* 900
  (photo: J. Schulman B.V)

Plate 5
21 Basse?: Edward VI coronation, 1547. Cast, 62 mm.   *AV* ——
  AR 3200
22 Hilliard?: James I peace with Spain, 1604.   *a AV* ——
  37 mm. *a* struck; *b* cast   *AR* 600
  b AR 150
23 Anthony?: James I coronation, 1603. 29 mm.   *AR* 600
24 Anthony?: Henry Prince of Wales, 1612. 29 mm.   *AV* 1500
  AR 280
25 Anthony?: Thomas Sackville, 1603. 29 mm.   *AR* 150
26 Briot: Prince Charles (II) birth, 1630.   *a AV* 400
  a 30 mm.; *b* 24 mm.   *AR* 40
  b AV 250
  AR 30
27 Briot: Charles (II), Prince of Wales, 1638. 32 mm.   *AR* 280
28 Briot: Charles I, coronation in Edinburgh, 1633.   *AV* 1500
  29 mm.   *AR* 280
29 ?: Charles I return to London, 1633. Cast, 42 mm.   *AV* 9000
  AR 700
30 ?: Charles I return to London, 1633.   *a AV* ——
  a 44 mm. struck; *b* 43 mm. cast.   *AR* 500
  b AV 2200
  AR 220
31 Rawlins: Earl of Essex, 1642. Cast, 30×45 mm.   *AR* 550

Plate 6   £

32	Rawlins: death of Charles I, 1649. Cast, 41 mm.	*AR*	350
33	Rawlins: Charles I and Henrietta Maria, *c.* 1649. Cast, *a* 37×53 mm. wreath borders; *b* 33×44 mm.	*a AR*	550
		b AR	400
34	Rawlins: Charles II Restoration, 1660. Cast, 17×23 mm.	*AR*	90
35	Rawlins: Charles II Restoration, 1660. Cast, 19×27 mm.	*AR*	100
36	Rawlins: Charles II Restoration, 1660. 31 mm. (*rev.* leafless oak tree)	*AR*	200
37	Rawlins: Charles II coronation, 1661. 33 mm.	*AR*	350
38	T. Simon: battle of Dunbar, 1650. 28×35 mm. *a* original striking; *b* 18th/19th century restrike.	*a AV*	——
		AR	800
		b AV	450
		AR	200
		Pb	60
39	T. Simon: Baron de Reede, 1645. Cast, 35 mm.	*AR*	600
40	T. Simon: Scottish rebellion, 1639. *a* 32 mm.; *b* 27 mm.	*a AV*	1200
		AR	300
		b AV	800
		AR	180
41	T. Simon: Charles II 'dominion of the seas', 1665. 27 mm.	*AV*	——
		AR	550
42	J. Roettiers: Charles II landing at Dover, 1660. 57 mm. (*rev.* ships approach)	*AR*	800
43	J. Roettiers: battle of Lowestoft, 1665. *a* 62 mm.; *b* 56 mm.	*a AV*	——
		AR	600
		WM	90
		b AR	500

Plate 7

44	J. Roettiers: battle of Lowestoft, 1665. 77 mm. (*rev.* naval engagement)	*AR*	1600
45	J. Roettiers: peace (of Breda) with Holland, 1667. 56 mm. (*obv.* Charles II)	*AV*	2800
		AR	320
46	Bower: Charles II Restoration, 1660. 64 mm. (*rev.* Jupiter hurls thunder)	*AR*	1000
47	Bower: Duchess of Portsmouth, 1673. 28 mm.	*AR*	250
		AE	120
48	Bower: James, Duke of Ormonde, 1682. 50 mm.	*AR*	600
49	Bower: James II *c.* 1685. 43 mm.	*AR*	280
50	Dutch: William and Mary coronation, 1689. 44 mm.	*AR*	180

Plate 8 £

51	Croker: battle of Malplaquet, 1709. 47 mm.	*AR*	170
		AE	60
52	Croker: peace of Utrecht, 1713. 35 mm.	*AV*	700
		AR	70
		AE	35
53	Croker: battle of Dunblain, 1715. 45 mm.	*AR*	200
		AE	70
54	Croker: accession of Queen Anne, 1702? or	*AV*	2000
	Union of England and Scotland, 1707? 69 mm.	*AR*	280
		AE	70
55	Croker/Tanner: George II, Caroline and their	*AV*	3500
	children, 1732. 69 mm.	*AR*	500
		AE	170
		WM	90

Plate 9

56	Tanner: Royal Society's Copley Medal, 1737.	*AV*	700
	43 mm.	*AR*	70
		AE	45
57	Tanner: Henry Jernegan's lottery, 1736. 39 mm.	*AR*	22
	(*rev.* Caroline waters palm-tree.)		
58	Tanner: John Milton, 1737. 52 mm. (*rev.* inscr.)	*AR*	75
		AE	35
59	?: James II's fortunes, 1696. 26 mm.	*AV*	850
		AR	220
60	N. Roettiers: birth of Prince Charles, the 'Young	*AR*	180
	Pretender', 1720. 43 mm.	*AE*	70
61	N. Roettiers: restoration of the kingdom, 1708.	*AR*	220
	38 mm.	*AE*	90
62	J. Dassier: George II, 1731. 41 mm.	*AR*	70
		AE	20
63	J.A. Dassier: Alexander Pope, 1743. 28 mm.	*AR*	80
	(*rev.* inscr.)	*AE*	30
64	J.A. Dassier: Hans Sloane, 1744. 55 mm.	*AR*	270
	(*rev.* inscr.)	*AE*	80
65	?: Admiral Vernon, 1739. 29 mm.	*AR*	130
		AE	35
66	Kirk: Anti-Gallican Society, 1745. 35 mm.	*AR*	90
		AE	45
67	Kirk: Kirk's advertising token, *c.* 1750. 30 mm.	*AE*	55
68	Kirk: Thomas Snelling, 1773. 31 mm.	*AR*	80
		AE	35

Plate 10 £

69 T. Pingo: Royal Society of Arts prize, 1754.   *AV* 500
    44 mm. (*rev.* wreath)   *AR* 60
70 Stuart?: Thomas Fairfax, *c.* 1760. Cast, 28×34   *AR* 60
    mm. (*rev.* inscr.)
71 L. Pingo: George III, *c.* 1785. 40 mm.   *AR* 350
       AE 100
72 Turner: calendar, 1742. 42 mm.   *AE* 15
73 Burch: William Hunter, 1774. Cast, 81 mm.   *AR* 450
    (*rev.* large vase)   *AE* 220
74 W. Mossop: Henry Quin, 1783. 41 mm.   *AR* 120
       AE 70
75 Küchler: Battle of Trafalgar, 1805. 48 mm.   *AV* ——
    Gold and silver restrikes, hall-marked and   *AR* 850
    with a slightly smaller diameter, were made in   *AE* 280
    1966 by Pinches.   *WM* 170
76 Dumarest?: Boulton's medallic scale, *c.* 1798.   *AE* 90
    43 mm.   *WM* 40
77 Halliday: Stonehenge, 1843. 50 mm.   *AR* 110
    (*rev.* wooded landscape)   *AE* 60
       WM 30
78 ?: Linnaeus' plant classification, *c.* 1830. 49 mm.   *WM* 22
    (*rev.* 11 classes of plants).

Plate 11

79 T. Wyon Sr.: Battle of Trafalgar, 1805. 45 mm.   *AR* 400
       AE 180
80 T. Wyon Jr.: George III Indian Chiefs' medal,   *AR* 900
    1814. *a* 75 mm.; *b* 60 mm.; *c* 38 mm.
81 T. Wyon Sr.: Alexander I (Russia) and Catherine   *AV* 500
    (Oldenburg), Mint visit 1814. 35 mm.   *AR* 80
    (*rev.* Britannia seated)   *AE* 35
82 B. Wyon: Coal Exchange, 1849. 89 mm.   *AE* 75
    (*obv.* Victoria and family)
83 Pistrucci: Waterloo medal, *c.* 1850. 133 mm.   *a* 350
    a electrotype; *b* gutta-percha   *b* 250
84 Pistrucci: George IV coronation, 1821. 35 mm.   *AV* 500
       AR 55
       AE 22
85 Pistrucci: John Chetwynd Talbot, 1853. 37 mm.   *AR* 80
    (*rev.* inscr.)   *AE* 35

Plate 12   £

86 W. Wyon: William IV coronation, 1831. 33 mm.   *AV*   500
                                                          AR   60
                                                          AE   28

87 W. Wyon: Great Exhibition, Exhibitors' medal,   *AE*   15
    1851. 44 mm.

88 B. Wyon: William Chambers, 1857. 55 mm.   *AR*   150
                                                          AE   45

89 W. Wyon: Victoria, Guildhall visit, 1837. 55 mm.   *AR*   240
                                                          AE   100

90 L.C. Wyon: Joseph Paxton, 1854. 64 mm.   *AR*   180
                                                          AE   55
                                                          WM   28

91 J. Carter: Victoria, golden jubilee celebrated by   *AR*   45
    Flint, 1887. 37 mm. (*obv*. Victoria)   *AE*   18
                                                          WM   12

92 Bowcher: Boer War National Commemorative,   *AV*   400
    1900. 45 mm.   *AR*   28
                                                          AE   15
                                                          WM   8

Plate 13

93 Lauer: Rowland Hill, Penny Postage jubilee,   *AR*   180
    1890. 65 mm. (*rev*. stamped envelope)   *AE*   75
                                                          WM   50
                                                          Al   50

94 Bowcher: Franco-British Exhibition, 1908.   *a AV*   900
    a 63 mm.; *b* 51 mm. (*rev*. female figure)   *AR*   70
                                                          AE   30
                                                       b AV   600
                                                          AR   35
                                                          AE   18

95 Fuchs: South African War, Peace 1900. *a* 70 mm.; *a AR*   80
    b 52 mm.; *c* 44 mm.   *AE*   45
                                                     b, c AR   40
                                                          AE   25

96 Fuchs: Alexandra 'Princess of Pity', 1900. 70 mm.   *AR*   170
    'square'. (*obv*. Alexandra)

97 Mackennal: Olympic Games prize, 1908. 33 mm.   *AV*   900
    (*obv*. standing figure of youth)   *AR*   450
                                                          AE   180

			£
98	Mackennal: George V coronation, 1911. *a* 51 mm.; *b* 31 mm.	*a AV*	900
		AR	65
		AE	20
		b AV	170
		AR	8
99	John: Edward, Prince of Wales Investiture, 1911. 35 mm.	*AV*	450
		AR	35
		AE	300

Plate 14

100	De Saulles: John Pinches, 1905. 24×32 mm. (*rev.* inscr.)	*AR*	28
		AE	15
101	De Saulles: Edward VII coronation, 1902. *a* 56 mm.; *b* 31 mm.	*a AV*	800
		AR	25
		AE	10
		b AV	140
		AR	5
102	De Saulles: Winchester College prize, *c* 1901. 50 mm. (*rev.* tomb)	*AV*	500
		AR	45
103	Allen: Liverpool, Anniversary of incorporation 1207–1907. *a* 64 mm.; *b* 36 mm. (*rev.* sailing ship)	*a AR*	50
		AE	25
		b AR	12
		AE	6
		WM	4
104	Stabler: naval victory off Jutland Bank, 1916. 76 mm.	*AV*	2000
		AR	120
		AE	50
105	McMillan: Great War Defence Medal, 1917. 36 mm. (*obv.* George V)	*AR*	5
		AE	20
106	Preston: British Empire Exhibition plaquette, 1924. 78×50 mm. (*rev.* inscr.)	*AR*	60
		AE	35

Plate 15

107	Mackennal/Metcalfe: British Empire Exhibition medal, 1924. 51 mm.	*AE*	20
108	Mackennal/Metcalfe: British Empire Exhibition medal, 1925. 51 mm.	*AE*	20
109	Metcalfe: Prince of Wales, visit to Cape Town, 1925. 32 mm.	*AR*	70
		AE	15
110	Metcalfe: A.H. Johnson, 1925. 51 mm. (*rev.* interior of building)	*AE*	20

£

111 Doman: signing of the Armistice, 10th anniversary	*a AV*	1800
1928. *a* 76 mm.; *b* 32 mm. (*obv.* Cenotaph)	*AR*	50
	AE	25
	b AV	120
	AR	8
	AE	3
112 Mackennal/Dulac: Poetry Medal, 1934. 51 mm.	*AV*	500
(*obv.* bust of George V)	*AE*	30
113 Metcalfe: George V silver jubilee, 1935. *a* 57 mm.;	*a AV*	1000
b 32 mm.	*AR*	30
	b AV	170
	AR	4
	AE	50
114 Paget: Master Mariners' medal, 1936. 50 mm.	*AR*	350
(*rev.* armorial bearings)	*AE*	120

Plate 16

115 Bayes: *Queen Mary* commissioned, 1936. 70 mm.	*AV*	—
	AR	—
	AE	65
116 Tautenhayn: Edward VIII coronation, 1937.	*AR*	90
60 mm. (*rev.* crown)	*AE*	45
117 Metcalfe: Royal Society of Arts prize, 1947.	*AR*	65
57 mm. (*rev.* Society's facade)	*AE*	35
118 Vincze: Paul Vincze, 70th birthday, 1977. 57 mm.	*AR*	25
	AE	12
119 Elderton: Harold Glover, 1970. Cast, 51 mm.	*AR*	—

Plate 17

120 Appleby: 'Medals Today' (Exhibition), 1973.	*AR*	28
27 mm.	*AE*	10
121 Osman: Queens Award Medal, 1973. Cast,	*AR*	28
24×25 mm.		
122 Stieger: 'Food Furrows', 1982. Cast, 66×71 mm.	*AE*	*
123 Dutton: 'Torridon Loch', 1974. Cast, 83 mm.	*AE*	45
(*rev.* plain) (photo: R. Dutton)		
124 Dutton: 'Sheep Moor II', 1982. Cast, 78 mm.	*AE*	*
(photo: R. Dutton)		

Plate 18

125 Stieger: British Association for the Advancement	*AR*	40
of Science, 1981. Cast, 49 mm.		
126 Chadwick: 'Diamond Head', 1984. Cast, 74 mm.	*AE*	*
127 Elderton: Anna Pavlova, 1984. Cast, 85 mm.	*AE*	130

Plate 19
			£
128	Elderton: John Lennon, 1980. Cast, 85 mm. (*rev.* Lennon stg.) (photo: R. Elderton)	*AE*	95
129	Leete: 'Theatre', 1985. Cast, 57×75 mm.	*AE*	*
130	McAdam: Picasso, 1981. Cast, 73×88 mm.	*AE*	*

Plate 20
131	Searle: Charles Dickens, 1984. Cast, 69 mm.	*AE*	*
132	Finlay: 'Terror/Virtue', 1984. Cast, 54 mm.	*AE*	*
133	Pennell: 'A Tree for Me', 1985. Cast, 49 mm.	*AE*	*
134	Rizzello: 'Dolphin', 1985. Cast, 85×97 mm.	*AE*	*

Plate 21
135	Anthony?: Anne of Denmark coronation? 1603. 29 mm.	*AV*	—
		AR	600
136	Balfour?: Charles II coronation (at Scone Palace), 1651. Cast, 32 mm.	*AV*	1800
		AR	800
137	T. Simon: Charles II coronation, 1661. 29 mm.	*AV*	1300
		AR	180
138	J. Roettiers: James II coronation, 1685. 34 mm.	*AV*	1500
		AR	150
		AE	120
139	J. Roettiers: Mary of Modena coronation, 1685. 34 mm.	*AV*	1800
		AR	190
140	J. Roettiers: William and Mary coronation, 1689. 35 mm.	*AV*	1200
		AR	150
141	Croker: Anne coronation, 1702. 35 mm.	*AV*	750
		AR	75
		AE	50
142	Croker: George I coronation, 1714. 34 mm.	*AV*	800
		AR	75
		AE	50
143	Croker: Caroline coronation, 1727. 34 mm.	*AV*	1200
		AR	90
		AE	70
144	Natter: George III coronation, 1761. 34 mm.	*AV*	1200
		AR	200
		AE	120
145	Natter: Charlotte coronation, 1761. 34 mm.	*AV*	1800
		AR	220
		AE	150
146	Pistrucci: Victoria coronation, 1838. 36 mm.	*Pt*	850
		AV	550
		AR	85
		AE	45

Plate 22   £

147   Metcalfe: George VI coronation, 1937. *a* 57 mm.;   *a AV* 1000
      b 30 mm.   *AR*   25
                                                                  b AV   160
                                                                   AR   4
                                                                   AE   2

148   Vestner: George I coronation, 1714. 44 mm.   *AR*   350
                                                                   AE   120

149   ?: George II coronation, 1727. 24 mm.   *AE*   25

150   ? (after Natter): George III coronation, 1761.   *AR*   65
      33 mm.   *AE*   25

151   L.E. Pinches: Edward VIII coronation, 1937.   *AV*   90
      28 mm.   *AR*   12

152   De Saulles: Victoria diamond jubilee, 1897.   *a AV*   800
      a 56 mm.; *b* 26 mm.   *AR*   25
                                                                   AE   10
                                                                  b AV   110
                                                                   AR   4

153   Bower: James II accession, 1685. 29 mm.   *AR*   50

154   Vestner: George I accession, 1714. 44 mm.   *AR*   350

155   Regnier: Charles I – Henrietta Maria, marriage   *AV*   750
      1625. 23 mm.   *AR*   45

156   J. Roettiers: Charles II and Catherine, marriage   *AR*   150
      1662. 33 mm.   *AE*   80

157   ?: Charles II and Catherine, marriage 1662.   *AR*   60
      Cast, 20×30 mm.

158   J.S. & A.B. Wyon: Leopold Duke of Albany –   *AR*   170
      Helena, marriage 1882. 64 mm.   *AE*   40

Plate 23

159   Smeltzing: birth of Prince James, the 'Old   *AR*   550
      Pretender', 1688. 60 mm.   *WM*   80

160   T. Pingo?: Prince George (IV), birth 1762. 29 mm.   *AR*   90
                                                                   AE   35

161   L.C. Wyon: Princess Victoria, 1850. 32 mm.   *AR*   110
      (*rev.* inscr.)   *AE*   40

162   Wahl: George II, visit to Hanover, 1729. 53 mm.   *AR*   1200

163   Searle: Edward VII & Alexandra, visit to the City   *AE*   80
      of London, 1902. 76 mm.

164   ?: George (VI) and Mary, Colonial tour 1900–01.   *AE*   15
      27 mm.

Plate 24

165   Bijlaer: defeat of the Spanish Armada, 1588.   *AV*   —
      52 mm.   *AR*   800

£

166	Dutch: Gunpowder Plot, 1605. 30 mm.	*AR* 120
		AE 45
167	T. Simon?: John Lilburne, trial and acquittal,	*AR* 220
	1649. 34 mm.	*AE* 120
168	Dutch?: Oliver Cromwell, *c.* 1655. 47 mm.	*AV* 2500
		AR 600
		Pb 80
169	Bower: Popish Plot, 1678. 36 mm.	*AR* 170
	(*obv.* janiformed head)	*WM* 55
170	Bower: murder of Sir Edmundbury Godfrey,	*AR* 110
	1678. 39 mm.	
171	Bower: murder of Sir Edmundbury Godfrey,	*AR* 110
	1678. 39 mm.	
172	Bower: murder of Sir Edmundbury Godfrey,	*AR* 150
	1678. 39 mm.	*AE* 80
173	Bower: Rye House Plot, 1683. 46 mm.	*AR* 500
174	Bower: Monmouth Rebellion, 1685. 50 mm.	*AR* 700
		WM 80
175	Smeltzing?: Monmouth Rebellion, 1685. 49 mm.	*AR* 700
		WM 80
176	Arondeaux: Monmouth and Argyle beheaded,	*AR* 450
	1685. 61 mm. (*obv.* James II)	

Plate 25

177	Smeltzing: anti-Christian Confederacy, 1688.	*AR* 300
	37 mm.	*WM* 70
178	Bower?: birth of Prince James, the 'Old	*AR* 190
	Pretender', 1688. 37 mm.	*AE* 90
179	Smeltzing: flight of James II, 1689. 49 mm.	*AR* 500
		AE 150
		WM 80
180	Müller: security of Britain, 1689. 55 mm.	*AR* 220
		AE 100
		WM 55
181	Wermuth?: peace of Utrecht, 1713. 43 mm.	*AR* 220
		WM 90
182	Wermuth?: John Law, 1720. 34 mm.	*AR* 280
		WM 120
183	?: Robert Walpole, 1741. 37 mm.	*AR* 140
		AE 30
184	Roche: resignation of Robert Walpole, 1742.	*AE* 40
	37 mm.	*Pb* 30
185	?: John Wilkes, 1768.	*AE* 12
186	?: 'Madame' D'Éon, 1777. 40 mm. (*rev.* inscr.)	*AR* 320
		AE 200

£

187 Whitley: French Republicanism, 1795. 49 mm. *WM* 50

Plate 26
188 ?: Beggars' Benison Club, *c.* 1826. 34 mm. *AR* 70
189 ?: London Pitt Club, *c.* 1808. 40×48 mm. *AV* 700
    (N.B. Portrait should be intact) *AR* 80
190 ?: Suffolk Pitt Club, 1821. 35 mm. (*rev.* inscr.) *AR* 70
191 Webb: William Wilberforce, 1807. 53 mm. *AR* 170
  AE 55
192 ?: Covent Garden Theatre, 'old price' riots, 1809. *WM* 120
    42 mm.
193 T. Wyon Sr.: John Hanson, 1810. 42 mm. *AR* 120
  AE 55
  WM 35
194 ?: Peterloo massacre, 1819. 63 mm. *WM* 90
195 Geoghegen: Daniel O'Connell, 1847. 51 mm. *AE* 35
  WM 20
196 ?: Reform Bill, 1832. 34×35 mm. (*rev.* inscr.) *WM* 30
197 Halliday?: Colonial slavery abolished, 1834. *AR* 220
    41 mm. (*obv.* William IV std.) *AE* 70
  WM 45

Plate 27
198 Allen & Moore: Lord John Russell, 1848. 31 mm. *AE* 60
  WM 35
199 L.C. Wyon: William Gladstone, 70th birthday, *AR* 60
    1879. 44 mm. (*rev.* inscr.) *AE* 25
200 Ottley: Benjamin Disraeli, 1881. 41 mm. (*rev.* *WM* 55
    inscr.)
201 Fray: Joseph Chamberlain, 1906. 75 mm. *AR* 70
    (*rev.* inscr.) *AE* 28
202 Bowcher: David Lloyd George, 1917. *a* 65 mm.; *aAR* 110
    b 45 mm. *AE* 50
  bAR 35
  AE 18
203 Goetz: Roger Casement, 1916. Cast, 58 mm. *Fe* 45
204 Metcalfe/Paget: British Empire Union, 1928. *AV* 150
    33 mm.
205 Metcalfe/Doman: British Empire Union, 1929. *AR* 45
    33 mm. *AE* 8

Plate 28
206 Bijlaer: naval action against Spain, 1596. 52 mm. *AR* 700
    (*obv.* three shields)

			£
207	Bijlaer: battle of Turnhout, 1597. 51 mm. (*rev.* views of nine towns)	*AR*	700
208	Rawlins: Earl of Essex, 1642. Cast, *a* 38×54 mm. wreath borders; *b* 27×38 mm.	*a AR*	600
		b AV	1200
		AR	400
209	T. Simon: General Fairfax, 1645. Cast, *a* 28×34 mm.; *b* 20×25 mm.	*a AR*	320
		b AV	650
		AR	160
210	?: Sir William Waller, 1643. Cast, 28×35 mm.	*AR*	450
211	Hautsch: Ireland pacified, 1691. 41 mm.	*AR*	250
		AE	90
		WM	55
212	Boskam: battle of La Hogue, 1692. 56 mm.	*AR*	450
213	Müller?: battle of Vigo Bay, 1702, 41 mm. (*obv.* Victory with crown)	*AR*	280
		AE	120
		WM	60
214	Hautsch: successes of Prince Eugene and the Duke of Marlborough, 1710. 44 mm. (*rev.* landscape scenes)	*AR*	280
		WM	65
215	Hautsch: attempted Jacobite invasion of Scotland, 1708. 40 mm.	*AR*	180
		AE	80
		WM	50
216	(German?): attempted Jacobite invasions of 1708 and 1716. 33 mm.	*AR*	400
217	?: capture of Portobello and Fort Chagre, 1739–40. 37 mm.	*AR*	160
		AE	50
218	?: Jacobite rebellion defeated at Culloden, 1746. 31 mm.	*AE*	45

Plate 29

219	?: Jacobite legitimacy of succession, 1749. 33 mm.	*AR*	450
		AE	150
220	Kirk: Montreal taken, 1760. 41 mm. (*rev.* river god reclining)	*AR*	280
		AE	120
221	T. Pingo: Louisburg taken, 1758. 44 mm. (*rev.* batteries bombard fleet)	*AV*	9000
		AR	1100
		AE	300
222	L. Pingo: siege of Gibraltar, 1783. 59 mm. (*obv.* inscr.)	*AR*	400
		AE	180
		WM	75
223	Abramson: Battle of Trafalgar, 1805. 40 mm.	*AR*	180
		AE	90
		WM	70

			£
224	Küchler: Battle of the Nile, 1798. 47 mm.	*AV*	8000
		AR	500
		AE	90
225	L. Brenet/Gérard: capture of Algiers, 1816.	*AR*	80
	41 mm.	*AE*	25
		WM	12
226	Allen & Moore: Charles Napier, 1854. 44 mm.	*AE*	90
		WM	60
227	?: Lord Baden-Powell, 1900. 25 mm. (*rev.* inscr.)	*AR*	18
228	Fuchs: General George White, 1900. 31 mm.	*AR*	20
	(*rev.* inscr.)	*AE*	12
229	Legastelois: Lord Kitchener, 1916. *a* 68 mm.;	*a AR*	60
	b 45 mm.; *c* 34 mm.	*AE*	22
		b,c AR	18
		AE	12
230	?: Wakefield prisoner-of-war camp, 1915. 31 mm.	*AE*	40

Plate 30

231	Bowcher: William Shakespeare, 1911. 44 mm.	*AV*	450
		AR	40
		AE	25
232	Stothard: Lord Byron, 1824. 64 mm.	*AR*	280
		AE	90
233	L.C. Wyon: William Wordsworth, 1848. 36 mm.	*AR*	45
	(*rev.* inscr.)	*AE*	18
234	?: George F. Handel, 1784. 32 mm. (*rev.* inscr.)	*AV*	450
		AR	60
		AE	30
235	Kirk: Joshua Reynolds, 1773. 31 mm.	*AR*	100
		AE	45
236	Hancock: John Philip Kemble, 1798. 53 mm.	*AR*	140
	(*rev.* inscr.)	*AE*	45
237	Bowcher: Henry Irving, 1905. 39 mm.	*AR*	35
		AE	18
238	?: Newcastle-on-Tyne high level bridge, 1849.	*AR*	170
	46 mm.	*AE*	65
		WM	45
239	Payne & Thompson: Clifton suspension bridge,	*WM*	25
	1864. 38 mm. (*rev.* inscr.)		
240	Ottley: Grand Junction railway, 1837. 48 mm.	*AR*	180
	(*rev.* time-table)	*AE*	90
		WM	45

£

241 Bain: John Rennie, Sheerness Docks and Basin opened, 1823. 64 mm.	*AR*	380
	AE	150
	WM	70
Plate 31		
242 Hancock: Joseph Priestley, 1783. 36 mm.	*AR*	120
	AE	55
	WM	40
243 Thomason: Phrenology, *c.* 1830. 73 mm. (*rev.* similar head, but facing)	*WM*	60
244 J.A. Dassier: Edmund Halley, 1744. 55 mm. (*rev.* inscr.)	*AR*	270
	AE	80
245 ?: Thomas Birch, *c.* 1750. 38 mm.	*AE*	90
246 Holloway: Peter Clare, 1779. 32 mm.	*AR*	90
	AE	40
247 Loos: Edward Jenner, 1796. 28 mm.	*AR*	90
	AE	55
248 J.S. and A.B. Wyon: Prince of Wales's recovery of health, 1872. 77 mm. (*rev.* royal family before St. Paul's)	*AE*	60
249 Elkington: Colonial and Indian reception, Guildhall, 1886. 77 mm. (*obv.* shield)	*AE*	60
250 Morgan: Francis Fowke, 1865. 58 mm. (*rev.* inscr.)	*AR*	90
	AE	50
Plate 32		
251 De Saulles: Edward VII Royal Society prize, 1901. 72 mm.	*AV*	—
	AR	250
252 T. Wyon Jr.: Royal Society of Arts, Isis medal, 1810. 40 mm. (*rev.* wreath)	*AV*	350
	AR	45
253 T. Pingo: Royal Academy of Arts prize, 1768. 55 mm.	*AV*	1200
	AR	220
254 ?: Ross Horticultural Society prize, 1825. 49 mm.	*AR*	65
	WM	22
255 J.S. and A.B. Wyon: Geological Society of London, Bigsby medal, 1876. 46 mm.	*AV*	600
	AR	50
	AE	25
256 Küchler: Essex Agricultural Society prize, 1793. 45 mm. (*rev.* wreath)	*AR*	70
	AE	25
Plate 33		
257 Küchler: Board of Agriculture prize, 1793. 48 mm.	*AV*	850
	AR	120
	AE	35

			£
258	Ingram: Devon Agricultural Society prize, *c.* 1837. 45 mm. (*rev.* farmscape)	*AR*	45
259	L.C. Wyon: International Exhibition prize, 1862. 77 mm. (*rev.* inscr.)	*AE*	30
260	J. Woodhouse: Trinity College Dublin prize, *c.* 1850. 39 mm. (*rev.* shield)	*AV* *AR*	320 35
261	W. Wyon: National Art Training School prize, 1878. 50 mm. (*rev.* inscr.)	*AV* *AR* *AE*	700 30 12
262	Ransom: London County Council, King's Medal, 1911. 31 mm.	*AE*	6
263	Bowcher: Alfred Willett prize, 1902. 57 mm.	*AR* *AE*	40 20
264	Macphail: John Hunter medal, *c.* 1870. 70 mm.	*AR* *AE*	90 35

Plate 34

265	Munsey: Cambridge University cycling prize, *c.* 1900. 52 mm. (*rev.* inscr.)	*AR* *AE*	60 40
266	W. Wyon: Royal National Lifeboat Institution medal, 1824. 35 mm.	*AV* *AR* *AE*	1000 280 30
267	A.B. Wyon: Royal Geographical Society Livingstone medal, 1874. 37 mm.	*AR*	220
268	Metcalfe: Everest Expedition medal, 1933. 51 mm.	*AR*	450
269	W. Wyon: visit to the Royal Mint, 1828. 38 mm. (*rev.* inscr.)	*AR*	600
270	J.S. and A.B. Wyon: North American Indian Chiefs medal, 1874. 76 mm.	*AR* *AE*	1400 75
271	?: Brokers' Pass, *a* 1707; *b* later issues of J. Milton, *c* 1790, and B. Wyon, 1830. 39–41 mm.	*aAR* *bAR* *cAR*	100 50 50
272	Kirk: Tylers' Company, *c,* 1770. 41 mm. (*rev.* plain)	*AR*	60

Plate 35

273	?: Vincent Lunardi, 1784. 35 mm.	*AR* *AE* *WM*	280 170 120
274	P. Wyon: James Sadler, 1811. 53 mm.	*AR* *AE* *WM*	350 200 120

£

275	Halliday?: Gloucester & Cheltenham Railway,	*AE*	75
	c. 1831. 43 mm.	*WM*	45
276	Ottley: New Channel to Newport, 1831. 51 mm.	*AE*	65
		WM	35
277	W.J. Taylor: Thames Tunnel, 1842. 42 mm.	*AV*	650
	(*obv.* Marc I. Brunel)	*AR*	90
		AE	28
		WM	15
278	Allen and Moore: The *Great Britain*, 1843.	*AR*	180
	51 mm. (*obv.* Victoria and Albert)	*AE*	75
		WM	40
279	Davis: Chinese junk *Keying*, 1848. 44 mm. (*rev.*	*AR*	100
	inscr.)	*AE*	40
		WM	20
280	?: Victoria Bridge, Montreal, 1860. 44 mm. (*obv.*	*AR*	120
	Edward, Prince of Wales)	*AE*	50
		WM	25
281	?: 3000th locomotive built at Crewe, 1887. 40 mm.	*WM*	20
	(*obv.* Victoria)		
282	Vaughton: National Aerial League prize, *c.* 1912,	*AE*	22
	38 mm. (*rev.* inscr.)		
283	Metcalfe: Carslake memorial medal, 1926.	*AR*	100
	51 mm. (*rev.* inscr.)	*AE*	45

Plate 36

284	C. James: 'Pigs Meat', 1795, ¼d token. 25 mm.	*AE*	20
	(*rev.* hand holds an open book)		
285	German: cat, *c.* 1770. 23 mm. (*rev.* owl)	*AR*	30
286–9	Loos: cat, *c.* 1810. 26 mm. (*rev.* inscr.)	*each AR*	50
		AE	30
290	?: 'Au Chat Noir', French token *c.* 1890. 28 mm.	*AE*	10
	(*rev.* inscr.)		
291	?: The Cat Club prize, *c.* 1900. 29 mm. (*rev.* wreath)	*AR*	12
292	Restall: Siamese Cat Club prize, 1901. 39 mm.	*AR*	25
	(*rev.* plain)		
293	Vaughton: National Cat Club prize, *c.* 1894.	*AR*	30
	39 mm. (*rev.* wreath)		
294	?: International Cat Exhibition, Germany, *c.* 1910.	*AR*	25
	40 mm. (*rev.* inscr.)		
295	S. Grün/H. Rivers: Cat Club of France, *c.* 1920.	*AE*	15
	40 mm. (*rev.* inscr.)		
296	Fountain 'Crouching Cat', 1988. Cast, 46 mm.	*AE*	30
	(*rev.* plain)		

£

297 Gallo: International Exposition Paris, 1933. 50 mm. (*rev.* inscr.)	*AE*	20
298 Lemoine: 'Two Cats', 1933. 50 mm. (*rev.* cartouche)	*AE*	25
299 ?: The Cat Club prize, *c.* 1900. 54 mm. (*rev.* plain)	*AR*	35
300 Virion: 'The cat, mouse and rabbit', *c.* 1930. 59 mm. (*rev.* plain)	*AE*	25

Text illustrations

Front cover, John: Investiture of Edward, Prince of Wales, 1911. (*see* **99**)

Back cover,

a B. Wyon: Zoological Society of London, prize medal, 1826. 77 mm.	*AV*	—
	AR	600
	AE	170

b George II, Royal Family 1732. (*see* **55**)

Frontispiece, W. Wyon/Domard: Great Exhibition, Council   *AE* 280
Medal, 1851. 89 mm.

Contents page, Fountain: 'Monumenta', 1985. Cast,   *AE*   *
40×68 mm. British Art Medal Society Issue £25

Acknowledgements, Elderton: Edward Elgar, 1984. Cast,   *AE* 120
95×101 mm. (photo: R. Elderton)

Fig. 1 Stuart?: Thomas Simon *c.* 1770. 38×46 mm. (*rev.* plain)   *AR* 200

Fig. 2 T. Simon: steel die, Charles II coronation medal, (*rev.*)   —
48×50 mm. (Mint)

Fig. 3 Richard Cobden, *c.* 1860. 'Bois Durci', 115 mm. (*rev.*   40
plain)

Fig. 4 Wellington's military victories, box-medal, *c.* 1815, 75   *AE* 350
mm. (containing 13 coloured card discs, by Edward Orme)

Fig. 5 George Vertue after G. Kneller: Abraham Simon.   —
Drawing, 142×191 mm. (BM P&D 1852–2–14–377)

Fig. 6 Bower: Anthony Ashley Cooper, Earl of Shaftesbury,   *AR* 160
1681. 40 mm.

Fig. 7 A. Nunzer: John Croker. Engraving from Lochner,   —
66 mm. *c.* 1744. (Mint)

Fig. 8 Croker: Mint approval for a medal, 1726. Drawing,   —
141×224 mm. (BL add. mss. 18757)

Fig. 9 Mint letter for the appointment of an apprentice, 1711.   —
(PRO Mint 19/3)

£

Fig. 10 Price list of Croker medals, *c.* 1720. (BL add. mss. 18757) —

Fig. 11 John Kirk's trade card, *c.* 1750. (BM P&D, Banks collection, 59, 103) —

Fig. 12 I. Carwitham: Thomas Pingo, 1741. Mezzotint, 150×188 mm. (BM P&D 1902–10–11–470) —

Fig. 13 Thomason: York election medals 1807. *a* WM 25
a Lascelles; *b* Wilberforce. 39 mm. *b* WM 25

Fig. 14 J. Kirkwood after L.C. Wyon: William Wyon working on a die, 1842. Engraving, 113×128 mm. (Mint) —

Fig. 15 W. Wyon: unfinished plaster model, 1851. 200 mm. (Mint) —

Fig. 16 L.C. Wyon: Great Exhibition Prize Medal (*rev.*), 1851. *AE* 65
75 mm.

Fig. 17 L.C. Wyon: Theobald Mathew 1847. 56 mm. (Mint) *AR* 110
AE 45

Fig. 18 Legros: Charles Darwin 1881. Cast, 113 mm. (without *AE* 120
reverse)

Fig. 19 Robert Arthur Johnson, Deputy Master of the Royal Mint, *c.* 1928. (Mint) —

Fig. 20 Percy Metcalfe working on a model of the Royal Society of Arts medal (**117**). (Metcalfe family archives) —

Fig. 21 Carter Preston: design for a League of Nations medal, 1924. (PRO Mint 20/933) —

Fig. 22 Bayes: unaccepted design, *Queen Mary* medal, 1935. (PRO Mint 20/142) —

Fig. 23 Kormis: Laurence Olivier 1949. Cast, 112 mm. (*rev.* *AE* 120
plain)

Fig. 24 notice for the distribution and sale of 1902 coronation medals. (Mint) —

Sources: I would like to thank the following for permission to use photographs of medals and relative material in their collections: British Library (BL); British Museum, Dept. of Coins & Medals; British Museum, Dept. of Prints & Drawings (BM P&D); Public Record Office (PRO); Royal Mint (Mint); and Sotheby's.

Royal genealogical tables

THE HOUSE OF TUDOR (1485–1603)

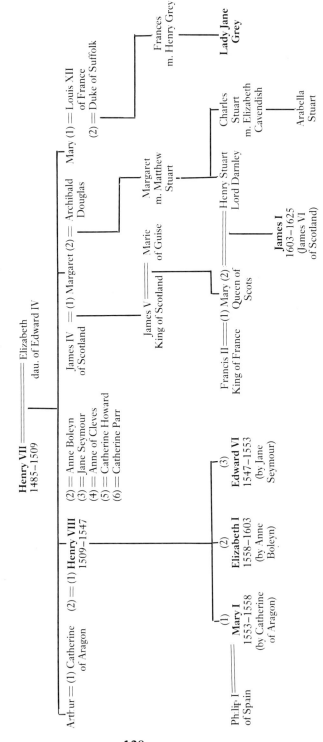

THE HOUSE OF STUART (1603–1714)

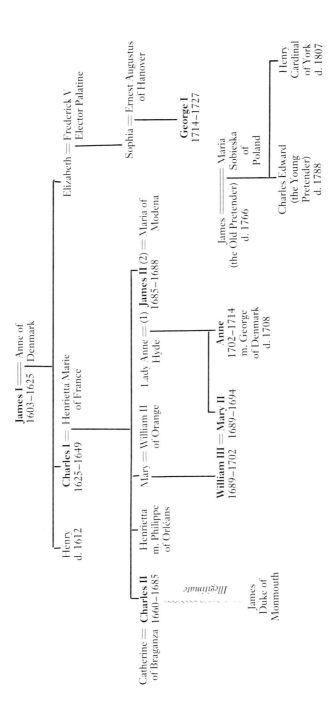

THE HOUSE OF HANOVER (1714–1837)

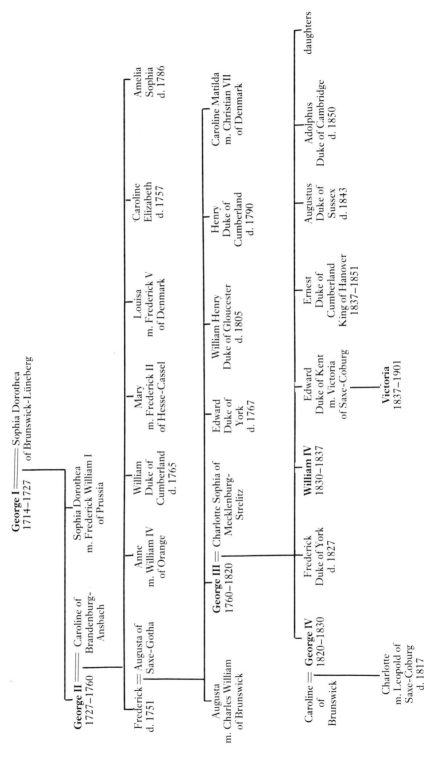

THE HOUSE OF SAXE-COBURG-WINDSOR (1837–)

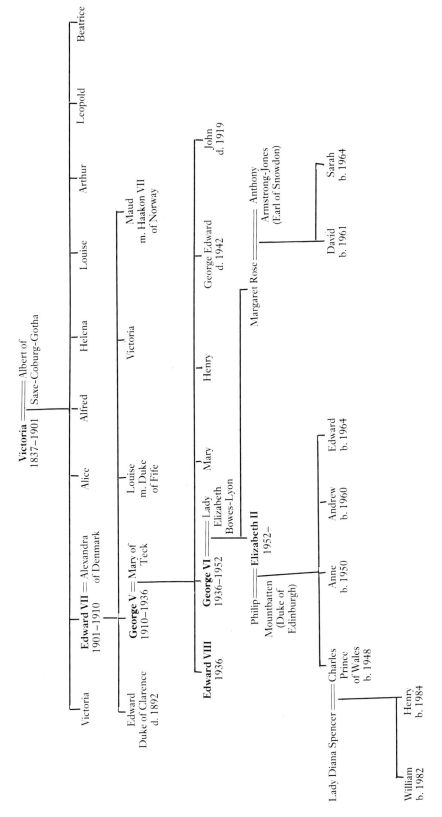

Bibliography

Allen, David G.C.: 'The Early Medals of the Royal Society of Arts', *The Medal* 3, 1983, pp. 1–4.

Attwood, Philip: 'Alphonse Legros', *The Medal* 5, 1984, pp. 7–22.

Betts, Benjamin: *The Medals Relating to John Law and the Mississippi System*, New York, 1907.

BL British Library (references are to the Department of Manuscripts).

BNJ *see British Numismatic Journal.*

British Numismatic Journal (BNJ), Proceedings of the British Numismatic Society, 1903 (vol. 1).

Brown, Laurence: *British Historical Medals 1760–1837* (vol. 1), London, 1980; *1837–1901* (vol. 11), London, 1987.

Carlisle, Nicholas: *A Memoir of the Life and Times of William Wyon*, London, 1837.

Croker Papers. Add. (Alchorne) Mss. 18,757, British Library.

Dictionary of National Biography (Compact Edition), Oxford, 1975.

Dutton, Ronald: 'How I Cast Medals', *The Medal* 4, 1984, p. 24.

Dyer, Graham P: *The proposed coinage of King Edward VIII*, London, 1973.

Eimer, Christopher: 'Sir Robert Johnson, The Mint and Medal Making in Inter-war Britain', *BNJ* 1985 pp. 169–91.
———*British Commemorative Medals and their Values*, London, 1987.

Evelyn, John: *Numismata, A Discourse of Medals*, London, 1697.

Fearon, Daniel: *Catalogue of British Commemorative Medals*, Exeter, 1984.

Forrer, Leonard: *Biographical Dictionary of Medallists*, 8 vols. London,1904–30, reprinted 1980; Index, London 1987.

Hawkins, Edward: *Medallic Illustrations of the History of Great Britain and Ireland to the Death of George II* (revised and augmented by A.W. Franks and H.A. Grueber) , 2 vols., London 1885, reprinted 1969. Plates, I-CLXXXIII, London 1911, reprinted 1979.

Hill, George Francis: *A Corpus of Italian Medals of the Renaissance before Cellini*, London, 1930.
———*Medals of the Renaissance*, 1920, (revised and enlarged by Graham Pollard), London, 1978.

Hughes, Graham: *Medals Today*, catalogue of the exhibition at Goldsmiths' Hall, London, 11–27 July 1973.

Jones, Mark: *The Art of the Medal*, London, 1979.
——— 'The Medal Collection in the British Museum', *The Medal* 6, 1985, pp. 8–11.

Kress, Samuel H: *Collection of Renaissance Medals at the National Gallery of Art* (based on the 1931 catalogue of the Dreyfus collection by George Francis Hill; revised and enlarged by Graham Pollard), New York, London, 1967.

Lochner, Johann H: *Samlung Merswürdiger Medaillen* (includes details of John Croker), Nürnberg, 1744.

Mechanics' Magazine. July 15 (p. 39), July 22 (pp. 54–55), London, 1859.

Medal, The. Journal of the British Art Medal Society, 1982 (No. 1) - .

Medallic Illustrations, see Hawkins.

Milford Haven, Admiral, the Marquess of. *British Naval Medals*, London, 1919.

NC, see Numismatic Chronicle.

Numismatic Chronicle (NC). Proceedings of the Royal Numismatic Society, 1836 (vol 1) - .

Newton (Isaac) Papers. PRO Mint 19/1–5.

PRO Public Record Office (all references are to Mint documents).

Royal Mint, Annual Report of the Deputy Master and Comptroller, 1870–1977.

Seaby, B.A: *Standard Catalogue of British Coins*, vol. 1. London 1984.

Spink and Son: *Numismatic Circular*, 1892–.

Thomason, Edward: *Sir Edward Thomason's Memoirs*, London, 1845.

Vertue, George: *Medals, Coins, Great Seals and other works of Thomas Simon*, London, 1753.

Wollaston, Henry: *British Official Medals for Coronations and Jubilees*, Nottingham, 1981.

Indexes

Medallists' Index

A listing of those responsible for the commission, design, engraving, die-sinking, sale or distribution of medals. The stated period of activity (*fl.*), which is given for manufacturers, as well as for those medallists whose complete dates are unknown, is not necessarily their only working period.

*Indicates those who did not work in Britain. References are to page number; those in bold are to illustration number.

Abondio, Antonio* (1538–91), 13
Abramson, Abraham* (1754–1811), **223**
Adams, George Gamon (1821–98), 35, 87
Allen, Charles John (1862–1955), 42–3
Allen (John) & Moore (Joseph)
 (*fl. c.* 1840–62), 38, 71, 78, 80
Angers, David d', Pierre Jean* (1788–1856), 39
Anthony, Charles (*fl. c.* 1599–1615), 59
Appleby, Malcolm (*b.* 1946), 54
Arondeaux, R. (*fl. c.* 1675–1702), 19, 65

Bain, William (*fl. c.* 1817–40), 80, 82
Balfour, James (1600–57), 59
Barnum, Phineas Taylor (1810–91), 80
Basse, Henry (*fl. c.* 1540–49), 57, 59
Battenberg, Louis (Marquess of
 Milford-Haven) (1854–1921), 78
Bayes, Gilbert (1872–1953), 50–1, 81, 91
Belli, Valerio* (*c.* 1468–1546), 13
Beresford, Francis (*fl.* 1712–22), 21
Bijlaer, G. van* (*c.* 1587–1602), **206–7**
Boehm, Sir Joseph Edgar (1834–90), 59, 61
Bonnardel, Hippolyte P.A. (1824–56), 35
Bonnetain, Armand* (1883–1972), 79
Boskam, Jan* (*fl. c.* 1689–1708), 19
Boulton, Matthew (1728–1809), 7, 28–9, 38, 77, 94
Bowcher, Frank (1864–1938), 40, 42, 72, 78, 79, 81, 89, 91
Bower, George (*fl.* 1660–89), 18–19, 64, 65–6
Brenet, Louis (*fl.* 1816–23), 78
Brenet, Nicholas Guy A.* (1773–1846), 77
Briot, Nicholas (1579–1646), 15–16, 57, 59
British Art Medal Soc., *see* General Index
Brock, Thomas (1847–1922), 59, 61, 92
Bull, Samuel (*fl. c.* 1707–15), 21
Burch, Edward (1730–1814), 28

Carter, Charles Fred. (*fl.* 1839–62), 83
Carter, Joseph (*fl.* 1884–1911)
 (son of C.F.C.), **91**
Carter, Lloyd (*b.* 1962), 56

Casella, Ella (*fl.* 1884–1911), 39
Cassioli, Giuseppe (*fl.* 1925–28), 90
Cavino, Giovanni* (1500–70), 13
Cellini, Benvenuto* (1500–71), 8
Cesati, Alesaandro* (*fl.* 1538–64), 13
Chadwick, Lynn (*b.* 1914), 56, 98
Chantrey, Francis L. (1781–1841), 33, 34
Cipriani, Giovanni Batista (1727–85), 27
Clarke, Geoffrey (*b.* 1924), 55
Collis, Geo. Richmond (*c.* 1835–68), 28
Croker, John (1670–1741), 20–3, 57, 59, 75, 76, 77

Dassier, James Anthony (1715–59), 24
Dassier, Jean (1676–1763), 24, 79
Davis, Joseph (*fl. c.* 1828–57), 38
De Saulles, George William (1862–1903), 42, 58, 59, 61
Deschler, Joachim* (*c.* 1500–72), 14
Doman, Charles Leighfield J. (*fl. c.* 1922–31), 42, 49, 73
Domard, Joseph François (1792–1858), 87
Drentwett, Baldwin* (*fl.* 1572–1619), 14
Dulac, Edmund (1882–1953), 49
Dumarest, Rambert (1760–1806), **76**
Dupré, William* (*c.* 1580–1640), 13
Durer, Albrecht* (1471–1528), 13, **15**
Dutton, Ronald (*b.* 1935), 55, 56, 102

Elderton, Robert (*b.* 1948),
 Acknowledgements, 56
Eley, Annabel (*b.* 1961), 56
Elkington & Co. (est. *c.* 1855), 40, 83
Enzola, Gianfrancesco di Luca* (*fl.* 1456–78), 12

Fattorini Ltd, Thomas (est. 1827), 38, 49
Fenwick, Arthur (*fl. c.* 1895–1937), 38
Finlay, Ian Hamilton (*b.* 1925), 56
Flanagan, John* (1898–1942), 63
Ford, Edward Onslow (1852–1901), 40
Fountain, Marion (*b.* 1960), **Contents,** 56

The following sometimes accompany a
medallist's signature:

Ad. vivum	from life	F. (ecit)	engraved
D	directed	Inv.	invenit (or designed)
Dedicavit	dedicated	Mod.	modelled
Del.	delineated (or drawn)	Pinxit	painted or sculpted
Des.	designed	Pub.	published
Dir(exit)	directed	R.A.	Royal Academy
Ed. (idit)	edited	R.M.	Royal Mint

General Index

Notes: references are to the page number; those in bold are to the illustration number. Some pages offer more than one reference to a single entry in the index. Royal societies and institutions are indexed under their royal title, whether or not it had been conferred at the time of the medal's issue. Royal personages who acceded to the throne are listed only by their sovereign title. Medallists have their own index.